Physical Characteristics of the Norwich Terrier

(from the American Kennel Club breed standard)

Tail: Medium docked.

Topline: Level.

Body: Moderately short. Compact and deep. Good width of chest.

Hindquarters: Broad, strong and muscular with well-turned stifles. Hocks low set.

Color: All shades of red, wheaten, black and tan or grizzle.

Coat: Hard, wiry and straight, lying close to the body with a definite undercoat.

Feet: Round with thick pads.

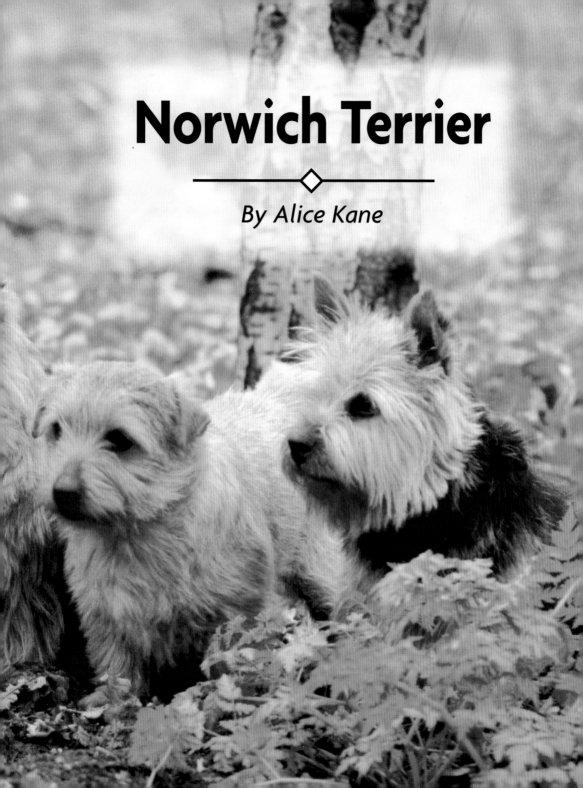

Norwich Terrier

◇

By Alice Kane

9   **History of the** Norwich Terrier

Unearth the origins of this endearing little terrier by reading about its beginnings, the colorful gents who helped promote the red dogs of Cambridge, its ratting ancestry, the history of the breed's name and much more.

23   **Characteristics of the** Norwich Terrier

Which attributes, other than his ever-erect ears, distinguish the Norwich Terrier? Why is he called the "perfect demon?" How does the Norwich fit into pet homes today? What do owners need to be prepared for? The author expertly answers these and many other questions that new owners have about this delightful tot of a terrier.

30   **Breed Standard for the** Norwich Terrier

Learn the requirements of a well-bred Norwich Terrier by studying the description of the breed set forth in the American Kennel Club standard. Both show dogs and pets must possess key characteristics as outlined in the breed standard.

35   **Your Puppy** Norwich Terrier

Find out about how to locate a well-bred Norwich Terrier puppy. Discover which questions to ask the breeder and what to expect when visiting the litter. Prepare for your puppy-accessory shopping spree. Also discussed are home safety, the first trip to the vet, socialization and solving basic puppy problems.

64   **Proper Care of Your** Norwich Terrier

Cover the specifics of taking care of your Norwich Terrier every day: feeding for the puppy, adult and senior dog; grooming, including coat care, ears, eyes, nails and bathing; and exercise needs for your dog. Also discussed are the essentials of dog identification.

80   **Training Your** Norwich Terrier

Begin with the basics of training the puppy and adult dog. Learn the principles of house-training the Norwich Terrier, including the use of crates and basic scent instincts. Get started by introducing the pup to his collar and leash and progress to the basic commands. Find out about obedience classes and other activities.

Contents

Healthcare of Your Norwich Terrier   **103**

By Lowell Ackerman DVM, DACVD
Become your dog's healthcare advocate and a well-educated canine keeper. Select a skilled and able veterinarian. Discuss pet insurance, vaccinations and infectious diseases, the neuter/spay decision and a sensible, effective plan for parasite control, including fleas, ticks and worms.

Your Senior Norwich Terrier   **132**

Know when to consider your Norwich Terrier a senior and what special needs he will have. Learn to recognize the signs of aging in terms of physical and behavioral traits and what your vet can do to optimize your dog's golden years.

Showing Your Norwich Terrier   **139**

Step into the center ring and find out about the world of showing pure-bred dogs. Here's the basics of how to get started, how AKC shows are organized and what's required for your dog to become a champion. Take a leap into the realms of obedience trials, agility, earthdog events and tracking tests.

Behavior of Your Norwich Terrier   **147**

Analyze the canine mind to understand what makes your Norwich Terrier tick. Potential problems discussed include digging, barking, separation anxiety, chewing and different types of aggression.

KENNEL CLUB BOOKS: **NORWICH TERRIER**
ISBN: 1-59378-334-5

Copyright © 2005 • Kennel Club Books, LLC
308 Main Street, Allenhurst, NJ 07711 USA
Cover Design Patented: US 6,435,559 B2 • Printed in South Korea

Photography by Alice van Kempen
with additional photographs by:

Paulette Braun, T.J. Calhoun, Alan and Sandy Carey, Carolina Biological Supply, Isabelle Français, Carol Ann Johnson, Bill Jonas, Dr. Dennis Kunkel, Bardi McLennan, Tam C. Nguyen, Phototake and Jean Claude Revy.

Illustrations by Patricia Peters.

The publisher wishes to thank all of the owners of the dogs featured in this book.

The Norwich Terrier is one of the smallest terrier breeds, a distinction which the breed shares with its drop-eared cousin, the Norfolk Terrier.

HISTORY OF THE

NORWICH TERRIER

Of the smallest of the terrier breeds, the Norwich Terrier suffers a bit of an identity crisis with his "cousin," the Norfolk Terrier. Until their official 1964 separation in their homeland, England, the two breeds were considered one and the same and exhibited together in conformation dog shows. The American Kennel Club followed up by separating the breeds in 1979. Even today, although considered separate breeds and with separate breed standards, joint clubs exist for fanciers of both breeds. This is true in the US, with the Norwich and Norfolk Terrier Club as the national club for both breeds.

Many years of discussion preceded the official separation, but members of the English Norwich Terrier Club persevered in their efforts and, in late 1964, England's Kennel Club divided the Norwich Terrier into two breeds—dogs with the prick-ear (erect) carriage retained the Norwich name and dogs with the drop-ear (folded over) carriage were given the new name, Norfolk.

To help you remember "wich" is which, the Norwich devotee will tell you to think of

The Norfolk Terrier possesses ears that fold forward and, like the Norwich, an alert and fearless outlook on life.

The Norfolk Terrier possesses ears that fold forward and, like the Norwich, an alert and fearless outlook on life.

a *witch's* hat, rising to a nice pointed tip—Nor*WICH*. A more subtle physical difference is the Norwich outline—broader, often shorter in neck and lower to the ground. But perhaps more important to the prospective family of a Norwich is the breed's preference for human company over that of other dogs, his easy adaptation to urban life and his happy-go-lucky nature.

Although the Norwich Terrier is of fairly recent origin compared to the pure-bred dog fancy as a whole, records of the breed's beginnings were not carefully kept. Perhaps this is due to lack of real evidence that the Norwich and Norfolk were planned breeds. Luckily, devoted fanciers of the breed, such as England's Norwich historian Marjorie Bunting, scrupulously worked to recreate its history.

THE BREED'S BEGINNINGS

It is assumed that this plucky little terrier evolved from English country sportsmen's breeding small red and black-and-tan terriers from other crosses they already owned, admired and wanted to perpet-uate. Historians of the breed do agree, however, that the beginnings of the type we now recognize as the Norwich probably came from Rags, a terrier-type dog owned by Mr. Jack Cooke of Brook Lodge, near Norwich, England, early in the 20th century. Rags was given to Mr. Cooke by his breeder, Mr. E. Jodrell Hopkins, who owned a livery stable in Cambridge and bred dogs known as Trumpington Terriers.

Rags's dam was similar to the Aberdeen Terrier of that time, small and dark brindle in color. She was mated to a terrier of

"Doggy" Lawrence, a dog dealer near Cambridge who bred and often sold small red and black-and-tan terriers to college undergraduates for ratting. These terriers were reportedly bred from crossing the old larger type of Yorkshire Terrier with small Irish Terriers. Norwich historians believe these small Irish dogs may have come from the protectively guarded terriers of Col. Vaughan in southern Ireland, who bred them down in size so that they could catch foxes going to ground in drains.

We do know that some of

Early Cambridge Terriers are believed to be crosses of old-style Yorkshire Terriers (larger than today's toy breed shown here) and small Irish Terriers (smaller than today's terrier breed).

these terriers eventually made their way to Cambridge. Rags, no doubt the product of these beginnings, was small with a profuse but hard red coat. Of great character and type, his strengths were evident in his progeny. No matter who his "mate," his red color and his superior type were passed on to all of his puppies—to the delight of his many supporters.

JONES AND TWO JACKS

It is through Jack Cooke's one-time employee, Frank "Roughrider" Jones, that the breed became better known. Very partial to the breed, Jones, after moving from the Norwich area to Market Harborough, became a dealer in Norwich Terriers. Hunting people visited the livery stables where he worked and fell in love with his perky red terriers. To fill the demand for puppies, he began buying litters for resale from his

> **THE CAMBRIDGE BETTERS**
> The Norwich Terrier was a favorite of Cambridge University undergraduates, who enjoyed wagering on the outcome of ratting contests. The unofficial record for ratting goes to a Norwich in Scotland who caught 300 rats and a couple of wild cats over a two-week period.

old friends in the Norwich area. He crossed hunt terriers with descendants of the coveted Rags, possibly also cross-breeding with Irish Terriers, Glen of Imaal Terriers and Yorkshire Terriers. His "creative" breeding stock was soon named after him, Jones Terriers. Many breeders got their first stock from him. Many of the dogs went to the United States, and Jones even sold a terrier to the King of Spain.

Red terriers were always abundant in East Anglia, and these earlier types could certainly have been the inspiration behind the Norwich Terrier. One of these well-known "pioneer" red terriers was Aylsham, a little dog rescued from the streets by Mr. Jack Read of Hapton Hall near Norwich. Delighted with Aylsham's type, he found the terrier's owner, purchased the little red dog and began using him in the breeding program of his Horstead kennel in the 1920s. He later mated

The Jones Terrier may have involved the breeding of this Irish breed, the Glen of Imaal Terrier, a rare breed that is longer and lower than most other terrier breeds.

PURE-BRED PURPOSE

Given the vast range of the world's 400 or so pure breeds of dog, it's fair to say that domestic dogs are the most versatile animal in the kingdom. From the tiny 1-pound lap dog to the 200-pound guard dog, dogs have adapted to every need and whim of their human masters. Humans have selectively bred dogs to alter physical attributes like size, color, leg length, mass and skull diameter in order to suit our own needs and fancies. Dogs serve humans not only as companions and guardians but also as hunters, exterminators, shepherds, rescuers, messengers, warriors, babysitters and more!

Aylsham back to Jack Cooke's strain (Rags) to build up his line. His famous dog Horstead Mick, an excellent stud dog, was behind many of the early show winners. In fact, Horstead Mick appears in many Norwich pedigrees today.

EVIDENCE IN OIL

While written records may not reveal the breed's exact beginnings, art gives us some inspiring clues. "Two Dogs," painted by Landseer, shows a short-legged, sandy-colored terrier with prick ears, strikingly like the Norwich. Also, a painting by Dyckmans (1811–1888) depicts an early Victorian group with a little drop-eared red dog, like the Norfolk, in its midst. Perhaps most surprising is Jan Van Eyck's "The Betrothal," painted back in 1430, which depicts a small dog exactly like the modern prick-eared, stocky Norwich!

A painting may have inspired breeder Jack Read. Breed historians believe that Read bred specifically to produce a dog resembling a painting he had seen of a small red hard-coated dog with straight legs, dark eyes and a firm jaw, not more than 25–30 cm (10–12 inches) high. Hanging in an inn at Wymondham, England, the painting belonged to a Mr. Nichols, who owned and bred dogs and was said to call his dogs "Norwich Terriers."

UNEARTHING THE NAME AND FUNCTION

The exact beginnings of the breed remain steeped in

The Irish Terrier, as it appears today, is a strong, long-legged breed.

COLOR CONTROVERSY

Jack Read, one of the earliest breeders of Norwich Terriers, drafted the first breed standard. He felt so strongly that red should be the only color that he resigned from the club when black and tan was officially accepted. Despite the color controversy, black and tan was in evidence very early on, probably in great part due to the Yorkie cross used by "Doggy" Lawrence.

mystery, and so too does the answer to the question: Why was the breed called the Norwich Terrier? Sometimes called the Trumpington Terrier, other times the Jones Terrier and, early in the century, the Red Norfolk Terrier, the breed was named by Roughrider Jones himself, as legend tells us. If the tale is true, Jones was once asked what these dogs were called and, as he had just come back from Norwich and planned to continue buying many puppies there for resale, he said, "They are Norwich Terriers!"

While some sporting owners believe the Norwich to be skilled in hunting fox and badger, most concede that the breed's greatest skill has always been that of a good ratter. In his natural home, East Anglia, farming for food was of great importance and a small ratting terrier was critical to warding off rats and rabbits. With his courage, skill and stamina, the Norwich Terrier was the ideal worker. There are stories of terriers easily killing over 100 rats in a day's work.

The name "terrier" may come from the French *chien terrier*, meaning "dog of the earth." The small, compact size of the Norwich enables him to do work in areas where other terriers simply don't fit. On the farm, he is known to slip into potholes, chicken houses and vegetable bins to catch vermin in places too small for most other terriers. Similarly, his size enables him to bolt rabbits and moles from drains, burrows and thick brambles. The game little Norwich will either dig out his prey or drive quarry out for hunters or hounds. He is expected to bark as he works so that his human partner will know where to dig—and, on occasion, know where to find and assist his Norwich! This independent and tenacious terrier is quite likely to take on

THE SADDLEBAG TERRIER

Near the city of Norwich, the Norwich Terrier was developed into a hunt terrier. He was taken out on the hunt, sitting in a saddlebag carried by the hunter on horseback, who followed the foxhounds. The terrier's head peeked out of an opening, and when the hounds holed a fox, he was put down to bolt it out of the den. Courage and stamina made him a formidable team member.

more than he can handle and may need a helping hand.

THE NORWICH TAKES THE RING

The Norwich Terrier has been as showy in the ring as he has been on the farm. England's Kennel Club officially recognized the breed in 1932 and, that summer, at a show in Richmond, England, Mrs. Phyllis Fagan's tan prick-eared dog, named Smudge, won Best of Breed over 14 Norwich, making 21 entries in 6 classes. By 1935, breed registrations were sufficient for The Kennel Club to offer Challenge Certificates (CCs), building blocks of a British championship, and the drop-eared Biffin of Beaufin qualified later that year.

In this pre-war period, ongoing controversies stormed regarding the breed's color and ear carriage. The newly formed Norwich Terrier Club, presided over by Jack Read, drafted the

Little Jane of Biffin and Biffin of Beaufin, owned by early breed promoter Mrs. Mainwaring. Biffin of Beaufin was one of the first Challenge Certificate winners in the breed.

first breed standard, stating that "The coat should be red with no other color." Although Smudge, the first Best of Breed, had been a black-and-tan, it took three years for that color to be accepted. Norwich historian Marjorie Bunting believes this was really about Ch. Manette, the top black-and-tan show Norwich, whose birth in March 1934 intensified the push for recognition of the color. Looking back at old photographs, there is proof that the color was almost always in evidence.

The decade after the war was a time of vision for Norwich breeders and exhibitors. New records were achieved, many of them by the Whinlatter kennel. Skilled in showing dogs and in the use of professional handlers, the Whinlatter Norwich Terriers were exhibited to perfection. Their controversial trimming was first protested but, when accepted by judges, became standard in the Norwich ring. In 1949, at the West of England Ladies' Kennel Societies' show, the bitch CC went to Whinlatter Allercombe Task—the first of 33 Norwich CCs won by that kennel. The most influential Whinlatter dog, however, was Ch. Whinlatter Charade, top-winning Norwich Terrier for 1959, top stud dog from 1962–1967 and the sire of a record 17 English champions. He

---

"I'M TOO FOXY FOR THIS HUNT!"
When hunting a fox, the popular red color and foxy face of the Norwich are definite drawbacks. Many a hunter (and hound) has been momentarily stumped as to which is the fox and which is the terrier! Many feel the Norwich is safer on the farm, worrying off the vermin, especially in the UK where fox hunting has been banned.

---

was responsible for the many black-and-tan Norwich in the 1970s, and, even today, he is behind the pedigrees of almost all of the show kennels.

The formidable Ragus kennel produced many champions by breeding to its foundation stock of lines from Ida Hardy and Phyllis Fagan. Most successful were their Norwich sired by Ragus Great Guy. In the early '60s, they used Ch. Whinlatter Charade, Ch. Whinlatter Cob and Half-a-Bob, giving them another winning run before the breed separation in 1964.

After the separation, the late 1960s saw an impressive win by Culswood Chips Girl, owned by Margaret Cullis. When only 6 months and 12 days old, she began winning three CCs at three consecutive shows in 10 days to become the breed's youngest champion. Her son, Culswood Chipwood, took a Best of Breed at Crufts, England's largest show,

The separation of the two breeds, with the drop-eared dogs being called Norfolk (shown here) and the erect-eared dogs Norwich, became official first in the UK, in 1964, and the breeds were shown separately for the first time at the 1965 Crufts Dog Show.

and, at the National Terrier Show that year, won Best in Show. Ending the year as Britain's top-winning Norwich Terrier, he was then imported into the US, where he became the second Norwich to win a Best in Show all-breeds.

Bill and Pauline Ford dominated the British Norwich Terrier scene in the early 1970s with their purchase of Whinlatter Caprice. Another impressive young dog was Ch. Withalder Locksley, who in 1970 at Crufts took his second CC,

was Best of Breed and won the Terrier Group—the first Norwich to win a Championship Show Terrier Group.

At the Windsor show in 1979, Ragus Gypsy Love, owned by Marjorie Bunting and Lesley Crawley and bred by Freda Bell of Templegrove, was the first Norwich to win Best in Show at an all-breed Championship Show. That same year, she was Britain's top-winning Norwich Terrier. From that time until today, the Norwich has continued a grand tradition in

A QUESTION OF EARS

No one can own a Norwich without at some point being asked about "the ear controversy." Right from the breed's initial recognition by The Kennel Club, problems began to brew. Early on, many breeders bred the prick-eared to the drop-eared, a policy soon abandoned as the resulting ears were often neither up nor down, but somewhere in between! By the 1930s, the breed had almost completely divided and talk began of official separation. Fueling the controversy was the overwhelming amount of prick-eared dogs who won CCs—in spite of more drop-eared dogs registered with The Kennel Club. There were even accusations of ear cropping!

No one type was the original or more correct, as both had been used in the early beginnings of the breed. By 1951, even a Crufts judge got into the fray, claiming difficulty in judging two varieties that differed in much more than merely ear type. Complicating the separation was the question of whether the breed should be divided into two varieties or two completely separate breeds. After many exhaustive years of letters, proposals and meetings between the Norwich Terrier fanciers and The Kennel Club, both groups officially agreed to register drop-eared Norwich as a separate breed called the Norfolk Terrier—not a variety of the Norwich Terrier.

At Crufts in 1965, for the first time, each variety was shown separately—aptly judged by one of the breed's pioneer show people, Sheila Monckton. In the UK, there are separate clubs for each breed. While the individual clubs continue to emphasize their separation, they do hold an annual joint rally, a match greatly enjoyed by members of both clubs, some who happily own, breed and show both Norwich and Norfolk.

Norwich Terriers continue to win prestigious awards at dog shows, such as this Group One win at the Crufts Dog Show in 1999, continuing the breed's tradition of success in its homeland.

its homeland as top show dogs, stringing together impressive wins and producing offspring that surpass their predecessors.

THE NORWICH IN THE US

The Norwich Terrier's original function in the United States was to accompany fox hunters to help bolt the prey that had gone to ground. They were bred to hunt in packs, and several hunt clubs utilized packs of Norwich Terriers on their hunts. The breed was officially recognized by the American Kennel Club in 1936 and was seen with both prick and drop ears until the two varieties were separated into distinct breeds in 1979, with the drop-eared dogs becoming the Norfolk Terrier.

Norwich Terriers performed equally well as show dogs in the US as in the UK. Int. Ch. Thrumptons Lord Brady was the country's top-winning dog for 1980, topping all breeds in the US. This amazing little dog won 148 Terrier Groups and 66 Bests in Show. Another English import of that time, Int. Ch. Ragus Lothario, won Best in Show all-breeds in the US.

After winning Best of Breed at Crufts in England, Culswood Chipwood was imported into the US and became only the second Norwich to win Best in Show all-breeds. He went on to sire many American champions.

Perhaps the most noteworthy Norwich in the US is Ch. Chidley Willum the Conqueror, owned by

Ruth C. Cooper and Patricia P. Lussier-Forrest and bred by Karen Anderson. On February 15, 1994, this outstanding terrier won America's most prestigious dog award, Best in Show at the famed Westminster Kennel Club show. For many Americans, this televised event was the first time they had encountered the breed. Within 24 hours, Norwich breeders all over the country were taking calls from viewers who were enchanted by this pint-sized personality.

Just three years later another Norwich came along, this time a bitch, Ch. Fairewood Frolic. "Rocky," as her many fans called her, was Top Dog of all breeds in the US in 1997 and topped her career off in 1998 with Best in Show at Westminster. A Canadian-bred Norwich, she was owned by Alexander and Glorvina Schwartz and handled by Peter Green.

AROUND THE WORLD

English and Swedish breeders have worked together for years, producing some wonderful Norwich in a cooperative effort to improve the breed. Swedish-bred Int. Ch. Cobby's Timothy Gyp went to England in 1989, the first imported UK champion, and won Best of Breed at Crufts in 1992. Top stud dog in that same year, his offspring, Elve Sir Tarquin, repeated the feat in 1994. Sweden's Ch. Cobby's Bun O'Honey spent a few years in England, winning top bitch of 1992 and then returning home to become top-winning Norwich. Her son, Ch. Elve The Viking, was top stud dog in 1995 and 1996. He was the third Norwich to take a top Crufts Group award.

The Norwich Terrier can be found in many other countries today, including Canada, Finland, Switzerland, Germany, France and the Netherlands. National kennel clubs are a good source of information if you wish to contact breeders in other countries.

Breeders of Norwich and Norfolk Terriers are not as feisty as the little dogs they breed. In some countries, like the US, the two breeds share a breed club as well as many fanciers.

"Clever, quick and courageous" aptly describes this dynamic duo of Norwich Terriers.

CHARACTERISTICS OF THE

NORWICH TERRIER

From the breed's early beginnings in East Anglia, to see a Norwich Terrier was to fall in love at first sight. Little has changed over the years. Family companion or able farm assistant, this is a breed with charm and know-how. And he knows it. Clever, quick and courageous, he will astonish you with his tenacity and amuse you with his sense of humor. But, above all, he will give you his heart, asking nothing more than yours in return...and, perhaps, a daily romp around the neighborhood or countryside and an opportunity to "oversee his property" and show off his agility and keen love of sport.

The idea of the breed was to produce a dog, game on the farm or in the field but agreeable and small enough to be a suitable household companion. Today's Norwich is that—and more. This is a dog lovable in both looks and personality. He is handsome and winsome. Rugged, yet so cuddly in appearance that you just want

The beguiling face of the Norwich Terrier belongs to an avid and able hunter.

A TRAINABLE TERRIER!
Do not let your Norwich "train" you! Independent thinkers, these bright little terriers respond well to patience and praise and prove happy, eager workers. Quite a few Norwich have distinguished themselves in obedience, tracking and terrier trials.

him to snuggle up beside you. His wiry, weather-resistant coat, in shades of red, black and tan, wheaten or grizzle, easily keeps him clean and fresh. His face is a wonderful combination of foxy cunning and childlike innocence. His coat is easy to maintain, requiring only regular brushing (a quick daily once-over is suggested) and baths as needed.

The virtues of the Norwich's personality are endless. While early admirers praised his work capability, his love of human companions and sensitivity make him an ideal family dog, adaptable to almost every contemporary lifestyle, be it city or rural. This breed is happy with the young and old, although, obviously, children should be instructed to treat their Norwich companion carefully, with kindness and respect. Likewise, inactive or older owners need to address the breed's love of play and exercise. Further, children and dogs should always be supervised together. Children must be taught to keep doors closed, gates locked, etc., for their dog's safety, and adults must ensure that these rules are followed.

Your Norwich may have a favorite in the family, but he will be kind to all, even newcomers, once given the opportunity to assess and sniff. He loves to investigate, often standing alert with a paw raised, waiting in anticipation for some excitement. While he would never attack a person, he is a good little watchdog, sounding an alarm when strangers venture too close. A delivery person should expect to be "announced" by your Norwich.

Small but not fragile, assured but not quarrelsome, the Norwich is amicable with other dogs. Nevertheless, he is a terrier and, since no one has ever told him that he is one of the smallest of

MEET THE NORWICH

Cute and clever? Without a doubt. But how about fearless and feisty? Independent? Digger? Chaser of small furry animals? All of the above. Call it "The Terrier Factor"—the traits most frustrating to pet owners, but prized by terrier breeders. These traits actually were incorporated into the first Norwich Terrier breed standard: "To sum up, the terrier should be a little demon."

That said, expect the Norwich Terrier, a hardy pint-sized package of action and attitude, to take over your home with the utmost charm, affection and happy-go-lucky sense of humor. As you continue to read about the Norwich Terrier, its care, training and breed traits, decide for yourself if you are game enough for this fearless little imp, indefatigable in his work and devoted to his human companions.

The Norwich is a very intelligent breed and easily trained, though the breed requires a trainer who is sensitive and responsible.

his group, he may well assert himself with bold play and an officious manner. He will take no nonsense if challenged, but if he meets the right pal, a great friendship could ensue, and you will have the fun of seeing your terrier at play. The Norwich is surprisingly tolerant of other animals, particularly if brought up with another species. That said, supervising your Norwich around any "small, furry mammals" is an absolute necessity. Norwich were bred to go after these types of animals, remember? One breeder tells the tale of a friend's terrier befriending a vixen, his "so-called foe," so you never know what to expect from your Norwich.

Any Norwich breeder will first tell you that this is a highly sensitive dog. A Norwich wants nothing more than to learn your language, tune in to your needs and anticipate what makes you happy. Look into the eyes of a Norwich and you will see the gratitude, wonder and joy that he takes in being your special friend. His faith in you will never waver, and you will want to deserve that trust by providing him with a life of happiness and well-being. Key to this is keeping him in the home, actively involved with family life. A Norwich should never be kept outside in a kennel. He may love the outdoors, but human contact is his reason for being. He will thrive mentally and

A PERFECT DEMON

The first official Norwich Terrier standard asked for "a perfect demon, yet not quarrelsome and of a lovable disposition"—the same traits valued today. "Demon" has been removed from the standard, but the Norwich is still expected to be "fearless." Fearless should not be confused with aggressive. A Norwich will not provoke a fight but, if challenged, will "give as good as he gets."

physically only if by your side.

The Norwich loves his human companions above everything else in life. Breed historian Marjorie Bunting tells of a terrier that, one wintry night, alerted his owner that something was wrong

HEART-HEALTHY

In this modern age of ever-improving cardio-care, no doctor or scientist can dispute the advantages of owning a dog to lower a person's risk of heart disease. Studies have proven that petting a dog, walking a dog and grooming a dog all show positive results toward lowering your blood pressure. The simple routine of exercising your dog—going outside with the dog and walking, jogging or playing catch—is heart-healthy in and of itself. If you are normally less active than your physician thinks you should be, adopting a dog may be a smart option to improve your own quality of life as well as that of another creature.

outside. When she went out to investigate, she found her husband, collapsed in the snow. There is little doubt that this alert, loving little dog saved the life of his family member.

Along with his sensitive nature goes a highly developed intelligence. The Norwich has often been charged with being "one step ahead" of his owner. Many can "tell time," waiting at the door or window when a family member is due home, or anticipating dinner by stretching out patiently in the empty kitchen right before mealtime. There are also other amazing stories of individual Norwich Terriers who have alerted owners to physical dangers and, in some cases, have saved lives. Your Norwich has a keen, alert brain and can learn almost anything that you take the time to teach him. He may also use that brain to demonstrate a sense of humor, to have a bit of irreverent fun with you, eyes gleaming to see if you can take a joke!

Because this is a highly intelligent breed, training and supervised play are crucial to getting the best out of your relationship. From the day you welcome him home, pet your Norwich frequently, gently playing with his feet and face, getting him used to being handled by family members. Enjoy some playtime with him.

He is a terrier! Play and handling are not only perfect opportunities to bond with your new dog but you are also stimulating his mind and satisfying his need to run off some energy. A busy terrier is a happy, easier-to-live-with terrier!

Like any other smart dog, the Norwich will quickly size up "who is boss." Setting boundaries right at the beginning will give him reasonable guidelines to follow and make him eager to please you. It is much like raising a child—a relationship of mutual respect is the key to building a strong bond. "No" means no. "Sit" means sit. Now! Say it only once. If you say it 100 times, your dog will learn to wait until you say it 99! So give the command and if your Norwich doesn't understand—or is being obstinate—gently but firmly enforce it. Above all, do praise him highly and exuberantly for making the "right" decisions. A treat, toys, hugs—whatever he loves best is his reward for being a good dog.

Positive reinforcement, not punishment, is the very best method of training a plucky, loving Norwich. Training is not a battle of wits, a challenge to see "who's in charge." It is the foundation of your relationship with your dog. And it may also save your dog's life. Responding quickly to a command such as "Drop it," "Stay" or "Down" has

PLAYING GAMES
Norwich Terriers love to play with their human companions. Fetching a ball will keep them happily entertained while you remain comfortable on the sofa. Tug-of-war games are not recommended, though, as they can encourage aggression in play.

saved many dogs from poisoning or physical injuries.

Perhaps the greatest bonus of having a trained Norwich in your home is the delight of a canine companion who has learned the fun and rewards of pleasing you. Terriers rarely make the list of "most obedient" dogs, and the Norwich is no exception. But don't let this little character fool you. He is perfectly trainable. If he respects you as his leader, he will love to please you and will delight in a working partnership as much as you do.

That said, keeping your Norwich busy is half the battle of

SMALL BUT RUGGED PACKAGE

Because of his small stature, the Norwich Terrier can do earth work that other terriers are too big to do. His stamina is unsurpassed and he can enjoy a 25-mile walk with no signs of flagging—if you are up to it, that is!

The Norwich is a rough-and-tumble little terrier, superb as a worker or "showman." He is one of the few terriers today that can go effortlessly from the field to the show ring—snaring as many vermin as he does show points!

own fun wherever he is. Of course, if you live in the country, your Norwich will be overjoyed to race up hills, splash through streams and sniff around. Of course, the areas in which your Norwich is allowed to run free must be securely fenced in; otherwise, he must be kept on a leash. His insatiable curiosity and love of digging can get him into trouble if not supervised. If you put your Norwich in a fenced yard, make certain that this talented little digger cannot excavate his way to freedom.

While the breed may have been born to hunt, today most Norwich Terriers scout out prey just for the fun of it. However, many people involved with the breed encourage their dogs' natural skills by participating in competitive terrier events. Depending on where you live, you can find tracking and earthdog events, scent hurdle races and agility trials to enjoy with your Norwich. Many Norwich have also distinguished themselves in the obedience ring, working all the way up to the top levels. This is a hardy terrier with attitude and unflagging energy. He is a "can do" dog and would like nothing more than for you to do it with him!

The Norwich enjoys an average lifespan of 12 to 15 years. While well-cared-for Norwich should be basically healthy and

keeping him out of trouble. Early on, the breed was dubbed "The Demon Dog," and a cocky Norwich loves nothing more than showing you how he won the title! Physically, they are tough, tireless little terriers, originally bred for action, and exercise is crucial to their well-being. A couple of daily walks if you live in the city or suburbs will run off some energy and stimulate a Norwich's natural curiosity. This creative little dog can find his not prone to illness, some terriers may suffer back problems and genetic eye diseases. Also worth noting, increasing numbers of the breed have been diagnosed with epilepsy and respiratory ailments. Advise your veterinarian that Norwich are said to be sensitive to anesthesia, something to be considered in electing surgical procedures not absolutely necessary. Additionally, some Norwich have had bad reactions to the leptospirosis vaccine component. Overall, however, this is a hardy and long-lived breed, thanks to the dedication of careful breeders who screen their

breeding stock and breed only healthy Norwich. In addition to genetic eye disease, breeders screen for orthopedic problems like hip and elbow dysplasia and patellar luxation.

As with any other breed, if you know your Norwich well, you will be alert to any signals of ill health. Appetite, thirst, activity level, toilet habits, etc., are all signs of your dog's well-being. As he gets older, watch for teeth, eye and ear problems and also swellings under the skin; more frequent vet visits will help detect problems early on. One of the benefits of regular grooming sessions with your Norwich is getting to know his body so that you can quickly detect any changes that may require veterinary attention. Luckily, this breed, like most other terriers, has a marvelous constitution, and you can expect your companion Norwich to lead you on a merry chase for many years.

DELTA SOCIETY

The human-animal bond propels the work of the Delta Society, striving to improve the lives of people and animals. The Pet Partners Program proves that the lives of people and dogs are inextricably linked. The Pet Partners Program, a national registry, trains and screens volunteers for pet therapy in hospices, nursing homes, schools and rehabilitation centers. Dog-and-handler teams of Pet Partners volunteer in all 50 states, with nearly 7,000 teams making visits annually. About 900,000 patients, residents and students receive assistance each year. If you and your dog are interested in becoming Pet Partners, contact the Delta Society online at www.deltasociety.org.

Start grooming your Norwich while he is still a puppy so that he learns to accept the comb and brush as part of his normal routine.

NORWICH TERRIER

WHAT IS A STANDARD?

Each breed recognized by the American Kennel Club has an approved standard that tells us what the ideal dog of that breed should look like and what we should expect from his temperament. A good breeder works to produce dogs that meet this standard, to assure that the breed you admire today will continue to thrive and improve in future generations. While the "perfect" dog has yet to be born, and probably never will, those breeders devoted to the Norwich Terrier work tirelessly to produce dogs that come as close to the ideal as possible. They cherish the characteristics that make their breed different from other terriers and are proud to tell you exactly what those are. The approved standard, meticulously put together by breed experts and historians, gives you a brief but all-important picture of the dog you are taking home with you.

While the standard was devised to protect a working terrier, a short-legged dog whose size, weight and stamina enable him to go to ground and pursue vermin, the charm of the Norwich Terrier is in his wonderful nature. Gregarious but not quarrelsome, at home in the country or city, he is a lovable terrier, adaptable under a wide variety of conditions. These are personality traits actually described in the standard, proof that those involved with the breed are as concerned with temperament as they are with appearance.

Dog shows are wonderful opportunities to observe ideal examples of the Norwich Terrier. In no way mere "beauty competitions," dog shows determine how closely each dog in the ring conforms to its ideal as described in the breed standard. Here you will see the Norwich as close to perfection as today's breeders can produce, not only in soundness and appearance but also in attitude. As the Norwich struts around the ring, he fairly reverberates with self-importance, daring the judge not to pick him. A thorough knowledge of the standard enables judges to know which dogs to pick.

The descriptive Norwich Terrier breed standard reflects the breeders' ideals and desire to perpetuate this fine, spirited little

Conformation competition revolves around the breed standard, and the Norwich Terrier that conforms most closely to the standard, in the judge's opinion, is the winner of the Best of Breed award. This Norwich went on to win the Terrier Group as well.

Norwich Terrier, showing the correct type and balance in profile.

terrier through the generations. Equipped with an understanding of this standard and an overall picture of the breed, the new owner can know what to expect from his Norwich and how to best meet his needs.

AMERICAN KENNEL CLUB BREED STANDARD FOR THE NORWICH TERRIER

GENERAL APPEARANCE
The Norwich Terrier, spirited and stocky with sensitive prick ears and a slightly foxy expression, is one of the smallest working terriers. This sturdy descendant of ratting companions, eager to dispatch small vermin alone or in a pack, has good bone and substance and an almost weather-proof coat. A hardy hunt terrier—honorable scars from fair wear and tear are acceptable.

SIZE, PROPORTION, SUBSTANCE
One of the smallest of the terriers, the ideal height should not exceed 10 inches at the withers. Distance from the top of the withers to the ground and from the withers to base of tail are approximately equal. Good bone and substance. Weight approximately 12 pounds. It should be in proportion to the individual dog's structure and balance. Fit working condition is a prime consideration.

HEAD

A slightly foxy expression. Eyes small, dark and oval shaped with black rims. Placed well apart with a bright and keen expression. Ears medium size and erect. Set well apart with pointed tips. Upright when alert.

The skull is broad and slightly rounded with good width between the ears. The muzzle is wedge shaped and strong. Its length is about one-third less than the measurement from the occiput to the well-defined stop. The jaw is clean and strong. Nose and lip pigment black. Tight-lipped with large teeth. A scissor bite.

NECK, TOPLINE, BODY

Neck of medium length, strong and blending into well laid back shoulders. Level topline. Body moderately short. Compact and deep. Good width of chest. Well-sprung ribs and short loins. Tail medium docked. The terrier's working origin requires that the tail be of sufficient length to grasp. Base level with topline; carried erect.

FOREQUARTERS

Well laid back shoulders. Elbows close to ribs. Short, powerful legs, as straight as is consistent with the digging terrier. Pasterns firm. Feet round with thick pads. Nails black. The feet point forward when standing or moving.

HINDQUARTERS

Broad, strong and muscular with well-turned stifles. Hocks low set and straight when viewed from the rear. Feet as in front.

A comparison of the Norfolk (TOP) and Norwich (CENTER) heads.

Norwich Terrier, showing the correct head in profile.

THREE STUDIES IN BODY FAULTS

Neck too short, high in rear, weak rear and straight shoulders.

Long back, dip behind shoulders, arched over loin and low tail-set.

Lacking substance, too high on leg, flat feet, straight in front and rear.

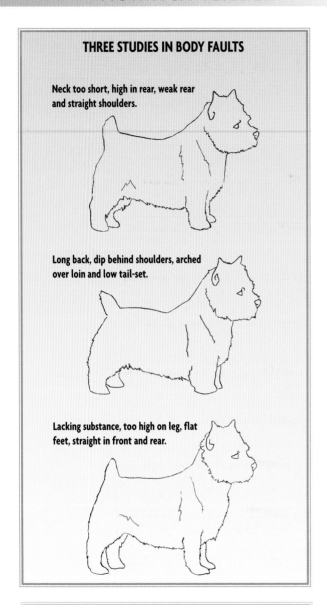

HONORABLE SCARS

The Norwich Terrier is a born hunter. The American Kennel Club standard states that, in the show ring, "Honorable scars from fair wear and tear are acceptable."

COAT

Hard, wiry and straight, lying close to the body with a definite undercoat. The coat on neck and shoulders forms a protective mane. The hair on head, ears and muzzle, except for slight eyebrows and whiskers, is short and smooth. This breed should be shown with as natural a coat as possible. A minimum of tidying is permissible but shaping should be penalized.

COLOR

All shades of red, wheaten, black and tan or grizzle. White marks are not desirable.

GAIT

The legs moving parallel, extending forward, showing great powers of propulsion. Good rear angulation with a true, yet driving movement. The forelegs move freely with feet and elbows the same distance apart, converging slightly with increased pace. Hind legs follow in the track of the forelegs, flexing well at the stifle and hock. The topline remains level.

TEMPERAMENT

Gay, fearless, loyal and affectionate. Adaptable and sporting, they make ideal companions.

Approved October 13, 1981
Reformatted March 23, 1990

NORWICH TERRIER

FINDING A BREEDER AND PUPPY

Assuming you have done research, observed some Norwich in action and studied the Norwich Terrier standard, you are ready to embark on the beginning of a long relationship, well over a decade, with a living, loving being. You should also expect to embark on a relationship with the breeder. Choosing a Norwich means committing yourself to the care and training of a sporting, sensitive, people-loving breed. A good breeder will and should scrutinize you to see if you are up to the job. Just as you deserve a breeder with ethics and the best possible reputation, the breeder needs to know that his puppy will have the family life for which he has been bred.

A loving relationship between owner and dog is all-important, but also of concern is how the dog will fit into your lifestyle. The breeder wants to know that you have the time and willingness to meet the needs of a dog that requires the love of his human family even more than he needs his own kind. Once the breeder

SELECTING FROM THE LITTER

Before you visit a litter of puppies, promise yourself that you won't fall for the first pretty face you see! Decide on your goals for your puppy—show prospect, performance-event competitor, family companion—and then look for a puppy who displays the appropriate qualities. In most litters, there is an Alpha pup (the bossy puppy), and occasionally a shy fellow who is less confident, with the rest of the litter falling somewhere in the middle. "Middle-of-the-roaders" are safe bets for most families and novice competitors.

"selects" you, you will be grateful for the relationship. This is the person you will turn to over and over again with anxious questions, small calamities and joyous milestones throughout your Norwich's life.

The American Kennel Club can refer you to breeder contacts. The AKC will advise you to contact the parent club for the breed, the Norwich and Norfolk Terrier Club (NNTC), which is the AKC-affiliated club responsible for both of these breeds. The club can then refer you to breeders in your area; NNTC member breeders are obliged to uphold a strict code of ethics in their breeding programs.

Dog shows are ideal places to observe the breed and talk to breeders who take great pride in their Norwich and enjoy the chance to share their enthusiasm with interested newcomers. Do visit with the handlers *after* they are finished competing. Showing a dog takes much preparation and

> ### FINDING A QUALIFIED BREEDER
> Before you begin your puppy search, ask for references from the breed club, your veterinarian and other breeders to refer you to someone they believe is reputable. Responsible breeders usually raise only one or two breeds of dog. Avoid any breeder who has several different breeds or has several litters at the same time. Dedicated breeders are usually involved with a breed or other dog club. Many participate in some sport or activity related to their breed. Just as you want to be assured of the breeder's qualifications, the breeder wants to be assured that you will make a worthy owner. Expect the breeder to interview you, asking questions about your goals for the pup, your experience with dogs and what kind of home you will provide.

The baby Norwich is not much bigger than a person's foot, yet his small size speaks nothing of the huge responsibility of dog ownership.

concentration, and the exhibitors will have more time to spend with you and answer your questions after the competition is over. Be prepared to wait for a puppy from your preferred breeder. Good breeders often have waiting lists—but there is a reason for that. They have good dogs and litter sizes are small. The wait will be worth it.

Choosing from a litter is an exciting, often emotional, time. While the breeder should help you select the puppy best for you, it is wise to know some of the physical traits to look for. A general rule in the Norwich Terrier is that any fault will get worse, not better, as the pup gets older. So if physical traits are important to you, make sure the young puppy is free of faults. Basically, look for a head broad in skull and slightly rounded. A fairly broad muzzle is desirable to avoid the snipy look as an adult. Eyes should be small, oval and very dark, as they may lighten. The ears of a very young Norwich puppy are often not erect and may even go up and down during his growth. The body should be relatively short and compact, with front legs straight. Plump (but not pot-bellied, as this may indicate worms) is better than thin in puppies, and lean pups could prove finicky eaters. The adult Norwich should have a hard, wiry coat and ideally weigh about 12 pounds.

Health clearances are important. You should check that the litter's parents are free of eye disease, cleared with the Canine Eye Registration Foundation (CERF). Also ask to see OFA (Orthopedic Foundation for Animals) clearances on the parents' hips, elbows and knees (patellae). Other OFA registries for the Norwich are cardiac and thyroid conditions, testing for problems that can affect many breeds. The NNTC has an active health committee that can give

This youngster already has the characteristic prick ears and alert terrier expression so typical of the Norwich.

you more information about health testing and genetic problems in the breed.

Temperament is, of course, what you will be looking for in a companion dog, and it makes good sense to tap the breeder's knowledge and intuition. The breeder has seen the litter interact and knows the bold puppy, scrambling for first dibs at human attention. Note also the timid puppy, sweet but needing a little coercion to join in the fun. The Norwich, male or female, is an inquisitive, outgoing breed, but each individual dog has its unique personality and approach to life. No one personality is right for all owners. The breeder can help you select the pup that will blend best into your own personal lifestyle.

The best indicator of your puppy's soundness, in health and personality, is the parents of the puppy you intend to acquire. Make it a point to meet the dam of the litter and the sire, if possible.

If the breeder has the puppies' parents on the premises, you should see them as well as the litter. Without fail, the dam should be available for you to see with the litter, though often breeders use stud dogs from different breeders. In that case, the breeder can show you photographs of the sire, preferably winning the Group in the show ring. The breeder can also show you the sire's pedigree and tell you more about him. Observing the sire and dam will give you some idea of what you can expect when your puppy grows into an adult dog. Just as in people, physical and personality traits are passed on from generation to generation.

Some Norwich breeders take pride in producing working dogs, capable of stamina in the field. Others happily see their litters off to good homes in the suburbs or city. The devoted Norwich breeders you visit have worked diligently to produce well-bred, well-socialized puppies. Now, their hope is to provide them with the best possible lives. When you have been "chosen" to take home one of their puppies, you will have all of their blessings and support.

A COMMITTED NEW OWNER

By now you should understand what makes the Norwich Terrier a most unique and special dog, one

PEDIGREE VS. REGISTRATION CERTIFICATE

Too often new owners are confused between these two important documents. Your puppy's pedigree, essentially a family tree, is a written record of a dog's genealogy of three generations or more. The pedigree will show you the names as well as performance titles of all dogs in your pup's background. Your breeder must provide you with a registration application, with his part properly filled out. You must complete the application and send it to the AKC with the proper fee. Every puppy must come from a litter that has been AKC-registered by the breeder, born in the US and from a sire and dam that are also registered with the AKC.

The seller must provide you with complete records to identify the puppy. The AKC requires that the seller provide the buyer with the following: breed; sex, color and markings; date of birth; litter number (when available); names and registration numbers of the parents; breeder's name; and date sold or delivered.

You can see how it's easy to lose your heart to a pack of baby Norwich charmers!

that may fit nicely into your family and lifestyle. If you have researched breeders, you should be able to recognize a knowledgeable and responsible Norwich Terrier breeder who cares not only about his pups but also about what kind of owner you will be. If you have completed the final step in your new journey, you have

THE FAMILY TREE

Your puppy's pedigree is his family tree. Just as a child may resemble his parents and grandparents, so too will a puppy reflect the qualities, good and bad, of his ancestors, especially those in the first two generations. Therefore, it's important to know as much as possible about a puppy's immediate relatives. Reputable and experienced breeders should be able to explain the pedigree and why they chose to breed from the particular dogs they used.

found a litter of quality Norwich Terrier pups.

A visit with the puppies and their breeder should be an education in itself. Breed research, breeder selection and puppy visitation are very important aspects of finding the puppy of your dreams. Beyond that, these things also lay the foundation for a successful future with your pup. Puppy personalities within each litter vary, from the shy and easygoing puppy to the one who is dominant and assertive, with most pups falling somewhere in between. By spending time with the puppies, you will be able to recognize certain behaviors and what these behaviors indicate about each pup's temperament. Which type of pup will complement your family

living sentient being that will be dependent on you for basic survival for his entire life. Beyond the basics of survival—food, water, shelter and protection—he needs much, much more. The new pup needs love, nurturing and a proper canine education to mold him into a responsible, well-behaved canine citizen. Your Norwich Terrier's health and good manners will need consistent monitoring and regular "tune-ups," so your job as a responsible

dynamic is best determined by observing the puppies in action within their "pack" and, as we've mentioned, drawing on the breeder's expertise and recommendations. Although you may fall in love with a bold and brassy male, the breeder may suggest that another pup would be best for you. The breeder's experience in rearing Norwich Terrier pups and matching their temperaments with appropriate humans offers the best assurance that your pup will meet your needs and expectations. The type of puppy that you select is just as important as your decision that the Norwich Terrier is the breed for you.

The decision to live with a Norwich Terrier is a serious commitment and not one to be taken lightly. This puppy is a

SIGNS OF A HEALTHY PUPPY
Healthy puppies are robust little fellows who are alert and active, sporting shiny coats and supple skin. They should not appear lethargic, bloated or pot-bellied, nor should they have flaky skin or runny or crusted eyes or noses. Their stools should be firm and well formed, with no evidence of blood or mucus.

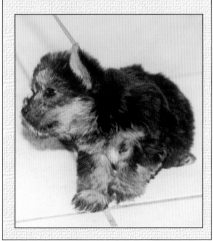

dog owner will be ongoing throughout every stage of his life. If you are not prepared to accept these responsibilities and commit to them for the next 12 or more years, then you are not prepared to own a dog of any breed.

Although the responsibilities of owning a dog may at times tax your patience, the joy of living with your Norwich far outweighs the workload, and a well-mannered adult dog is worth your time and effort. Before your very

The breeder provides cozy, clean living quarters for the pups and keeps a careful watch over the litter.

eyes, your new charge will grow up to be your most loyal friend, devoted to you unconditionally.

YOUR NORWICH TERRIER SHOPPING LIST

Just as expectant parents prepare a nursery for their baby, so should you ready your home for the arrival of your Norwich Terrier pup. If you have the necessary puppy supplies purchased and in place before he comes home, it will ease the puppy's transition from the warmth and familiarity of his mom and littermates to the brand-new environment of his new home and human family. You will be too busy to stock up and prepare your house after your pup comes home, that's for sure! Imagine how a pup must feel upon being transported to a strange new place. It's up to you to comfort him and to let your little pup know that he is going to be happy with you.

FOOD AND WATER BOWLS

Your puppy will need separate bowls for his food and water. Stainless steel pans are generally preferred over plastic bowls since they sterilize better and pups are less inclined to chew on the metal. Heavy-duty ceramic bowls are popular, but consider how often you will have to pick up those heavy bowls. Small-sized bowls will suffice for the Norwich Terrier as a puppy and adult.

THE DOG CRATE

If you think that crates are tools of punishment and confinement for when a dog has misbehaved, think again. Most breeders and almost all trainers recommend a crate as the preferred house-training aid as well as for all-around puppy training and safety. Because dogs are natural den creatures that prefer cave-like environments, the benefits of crate use are many. The crate provides the puppy with his very own "safe house," a cozy place to sleep, take a break or seek comfort with a favorite toy; a travel aid to house your dog when on the road, at motels or at the vet's office; a training aid to help teach your puppy proper toileting habits; a place of solitude when non-dog people happen to drop by and don't want a lively puppy—or even a well-behaved adult dog—saying hello or begging for attention.

The breeder and vet carefully monitor each pup's growth and development.

Sturdy easy-to-clean chew-resistant bowls are needed for your Norwich.

can be problematic in hot weather. Some of the newer crates are made of heavy plastic mesh; they are very lightweight and fold up into slim-line suitcases. However, a mesh crate might not be suitable for a pup with manic chewing habits.

Don't bother with a puppy-sized crate. The Norwich Terrier is tiny as a puppy and is a small terrier when fully grown, so an adult-sized crate is fine from the outset. A small crate, about 24 inches long by 18 inches wide by 21 inches high, will suit him nicely in the home.

BEDDING AND CRATE PADS

Your puppy will enjoy some type of soft bedding in his "room" (the crate), something he can snuggle into to feel cozy and secure. Old towels or blankets are good choices for a young pup, since he

The Norwich Terrier will accept his crate as his home away from home in no time. Crate training pays countless dividends in a properly trained dog later in life.

The three most common crate types: mesh on the left, wire on the right and fiberglass on top.

Crates come in several types, although the wire crate and the fiberglass airline-type crate are the most popular. Both are safe and your puppy will adjust to either one, so the choice is up to you. The wire crates offer better visibility for the pup as well as better ventilation. Many of the wire crates fold down for easy transport. The fiberglass crates, similar to those used by the airlines for animal transport, are sturdier and more den-like. However, the fiberglass crates do not fold down and are less ventilated than wire crates, which

CRATE EXPECTATIONS

To make the crate more inviting to your puppy, you can offer his first meal or two inside the crate, always keeping the crate door open so that he does not feel confined. Keep a favorite toy or two in the crate for him to play with while inside. You can also cover the crate at night with a lightweight sheet to make it more den-like and remove the stimuli of household activity. Never put him into his crate as punishment or as you are scolding him, since he will then associate his crate with negative situations and avoid going there.

may (and probably will) have a toileting accident or two in the crate or decide to chew on the bedding material. Once he is fully trained and out of the early chewing stage, you can replace the puppy bedding with a permanent crate pad if you prefer. Crate pads and other dog beds run the gamut from inexpensive to high-end doggie-designer styles, but don't splurge on the good stuff until you are sure that your puppy is reliable and won't tear it up or make a mess on it.

PUPPY TOYS

Just as infants and older children require objects to stimulate their minds and bodies, puppies need toys to entertain their curious brains, wiggly paws and achy teeth. A fun array of safe doggie toys will help satisfy your puppy's chewing instincts and distract him from gnawing on the leg of your antique chair or your new leather sofa. Most puppy toys are cute and look as if they would be a lot of fun, but not all are necessarily safe or good for your puppy, so use caution when you go puppy-toy shopping.

Like all the other terriers, Norwich have teeth that are big and strong, a bit large for the size of the dog's mouth. Terriers are aggressive chewers and only the hardest, strongest toys should be offered to them. Norwich breeders advise owners to resist stuffed toys, because they incite the breed's prey instincts and can become de-stuffed in no time. The

Before puppies receive any formal training, they learn life lessons from a very good teacher—mom!

TOYS 'R SAFE

The vast array of tantalizing puppy toys is staggering. Stroll through any pet shop or pet-supply outlet and you will see that the choices can be overwhelming. However, not all dog toys are safe or sensible. Most very young puppies enjoy soft woolly toys that they can snuggle with and carry around. (You know they have outgrown them when they shred them up!) Avoid toys that have buttons, tabs or other enhancements that can be chewed off and swallowed. Soft toys that squeak are fun, but make sure your puppy does not disembowel the toy and remove (and swallow) the squeaker. Toys that rattle or make noise can excite a puppy, but they present the same danger as the squeaky kind and so require supervision. Hard rubber toys that bounce can also entertain a pup, but make sure that the toy is too big for your pup to swallow.

inside stuffing in these toys can be dangerous if swallowed by the excited "killer" Norwich puppy.

Squeaky toys are heavenly for Norwich, as they resemble their favorite quarry, the deplorable noisy rat! It is best to use a squeaky toy only as an aid in training, but not for free play, as the toy won't last very long once your Norwich gets a hold of it. If a pup "disembowels" one of these, the small plastic squeaker inside can be dangerous if swallowed. Monitor the condition of all your pup's toys carefully and get rid of any that have been chewed to the point of becoming potentially dangerous.

Be especially careful of natural bones, which can splinter or develop dangerous sharp edges; pups can easily swallow or choke on those bone splinters. Veterinarians often tell of surgical nightmares involving bits of splintered bone, because in addition to the danger of choking, the sharp pieces can damage the intestinal tract.

Similarly, rawhide chews, while a favorite of most dogs and puppies, can be equally dangerous. Pieces of rawhide are easily swallowed after they get soft and gummy from chewing, and dogs have been known to choke on large pieces of ingested rawhide. Rawhide chews should be offered only when you can supervise the puppy. Rope toys offer good dental benefits, flossing the teeth as the dog chews, as long as the strings aren't ingested. Again, the rule for all toys is to monitor them and remove any that are in unsafe condition.

If you believe that your pup has ingested a piece of one of his toys, check his stools for the next couple of days to see if he passes the item when he defecates. At the same time, also watch for signs of intestinal distress. A call to your veterinarian might be in order to get his advice and be on the safe side.

An all-time favorite toy for puppies (young and old!) is the empty gallon milk jug. Hard plastic juice containers—46 ounces or more—are also excellent. Such containers make lots of noise when they are batted about, and puppies go crazy with delight as they play with them. However, they don't last long at all, so be sure to remove and replace them when they get chewed up.

A word of caution about homemade toys: be careful with your choices of non-traditional play objects. Never use old shoes or socks, since a puppy cannot distinguish between the old ones on which he's allowed to chew and the new ones in your closet that are strictly off limits. That principle applies to anything that resembles something that you don't want your puppy to chew up.

COLLARS

A lightweight nylon collar is the best choice for a very young pup. Quick-clip collars are easy to put on and remove, and they can be adjusted as the puppy grows. Introduce him to his collar as soon as he comes home to get him accustomed to wearing it. He'll get used to it quickly and won't mind a bit. Make sure that it is snug enough that it won't slip off, yet loose enough to be comfortable for the pup. You should be able to slip two fingers between the collar and his neck. Check the collar often, as puppies grow in spurts, and his collar can become too tight almost overnight. Choke collars are made for training but are not suitable for small dogs

The Norwich Terrier puppy coat will be softer than that of an adult Norwich, but somewhat harsher than those of non-terrier pups.

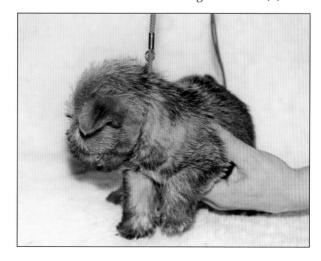

COLLARING OUR CANINES

The standard flat collar with a buckle or a snap, in leather, nylon or cotton, is widely regarded as the everyday all-purpose collar. If the collar fits correctly, you should be able to fit two fingers between the collar and the dog's neck.

Leather Buckle Collars

Limited-Slip Collar

The martingale, Greyhound or limited-slip collar is preferred by many dog owners and trainers. It is fixed with an extra loop that tightens when pressure is applied to the leash. The martingale collar gets tighter but does not "choke" the dog. The limited-slip collar should only be used for walking and training, not for free play or interaction with another dog. These types of collar should never be left on the dog, as the extra loop can lead to accidents.

Choke collars, usually made of stainless steel, are made for training purposes but are not suitable for small dogs (including the Norwich) or heavily coated breeds. The chains can injure small dogs or damage long/abundant coats. Thin nylon choke leads are commonly used on show dogs while in the ring, though they are not practical for everyday use.

The harness, with two or three straps that attach over the dog's shoulders and around his torso, is a humane and safe alternative to the conventional collar. By and large, a well-made harness is virtually escape-proof. Harnesses are available in nylon and mesh and can be outfitted on most dogs, with chest girths ranging from 10 to 30 inches.

Snap Bolt Choke Collar

Harness

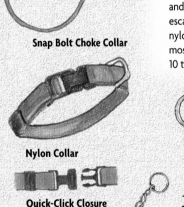

Nylon Collar

Quick-Click Closure

Snake Chain

Chrome Steel

Fur-Saver

Choke Chain Collars

A head collar, composed of a nylon strap that goes around the dog's muzzle and a second strap that wraps around his neck, offers the owner better control over his dog. This device is recommended for problem-solving with dogs (including jumping up, pulling and aggressive behaviors), but must be used with care.

A training halter, including a flat collar and two straps, made of nylon and webbing, is designed for walking. There are several on the market; some are more difficult to put on the dog than others. The halter harness, with two small slip rings at each end, is recommended for ease of use.

like the Norwich and sometimes are not recommended for terriers in general.

LEASHES

A 6-foot nylon lead is an excellent choice for a young puppy. It is lightweight and not as tempting to chew as a leather lead. You can switch to a 6-foot leather lead after your pup has grown and is used to walking politely on a lead. For initial puppy walks and house-training purposes, you should invest in a shorter lead so that you have more control over the puppy. At first, you don't want him wandering too far away from you, and when taking him out for toileting you will want to keep him in the specific area that you've chosen for his potty spot.

Once the puppy is heel-trained with a traditional leash, you can consider purchasing a retractable lead. A retractable lead is excellent for walking adult dogs that are already leash-wise. This type of lead allows the dog to roam farther away from you and explore a wider area when out walking, and also retracts when you need to keep him close to you.

HOME SAFETY FOR YOUR PUPPY

The importance of puppy-proofing cannot be overstated. In addition to making your house comfortable for your Norwich Terrier's arrival, you also must make sure that your house is safe for your puppy before you bring him home. There are countless hazards in the owner's personal living environment that a pup can sniff, chew, swallow or destroy. Many are obvious; others are not. Do a thorough advance house check to remove or rearrange those things that could hurt your puppy, keeping any potentially dangerous items out of areas to which he will have access.

Electrical cords are especially dangerous, since puppies view them as irresistible chew toys. Unplug and remove all exposed cords or fasten them beneath a baseboard where the puppy cannot reach them. Veterinarians and firefighters can tell you horror stories about electrical burns and house fires that resulted from puppy-chewed electrical cords. Consider this a most serious precaution for your puppy and the rest of your family.

THE GRASS IS ALWAYS GREENER

Must dog owners decide between their beloved canine pals and their perfectly manicured emerald-green lawns? Just as dog urine is no tonic for growing grass, lawn chemicals are extremely dangerous to your dog. Fertilizers, pesticides and herbicides pose real threats to canines and humans alike. Cocoa-bean mulch can poison dogs if they eat it. For other types of fertilizer, dogs must be kept off treated grounds for at least 24 hours following treatment. Consider some organic options for your lawn care, such as using a homemade compost or a natural fertilizer instead of a commercial chemical. Some dog-conscious lawnkeepers avoid fertilizers entirely,

keeping up their lawns by watering, aerating, mowing and seeding frequently.

As always, dogs complicate the equation. Canines love grass. They roll in it, eat it and love to bury their noses in it—and then do their business in it! Grass can mean hours of feel-good, smell-good fun! In addition to the dangers of lawn-care chemicals, there's also the threat of burs, thorns and pebbles in the grass, not to mention the very common grass allergy. Many dogs develop an incurably itchy skin condition from grass, especially in the late summer when the world is in full bloom.

Scout your home for tiny objects that might be seen at a pup's eye level. Keep medication bottles and cleaning supplies well out of reach, and do the same with wastebaskets and other trash containers. It goes without saying that you should not use rodent poison or other toxic chemicals in any puppy area and that you must keep such containers safely locked up. You will be amazed at how many places a curious terrier can discover!

Once your house has cleared inspection, check your yard. The Norwich is a natural digger and likes to practice his craft, especially outdoors in the yard when he's bored. The remedy is to keep him busy, keep an eye on his time in the yard and make the fence well embedded into the ground (at least a foot deep) and high enough so that it really is impossible for your dog to get over it. Check the fence periodically for necessary repairs. If there is a weak link or space to squeeze through, you can be sure that a determined Norwich Terrier will discover it!

The garage and shed can be hazardous places, as things like

A Dog-Safe Home

The dog-safety police are taking you and your Norwich Terrier on a house tour. Let's go room by room and see how safe your own home is for your new family member. The following items are doggie dangers, so either they must be removed or the dog should be monitored or not allowed access to these areas.

Living Room

- house plants (some varieties are poisonous)
- fireplace or wood-burning stove
- paint on the walls (lead-based paint is toxic)
- lead drapery weights (toxic lead)
- lamps and electrical cords
- carpet cleaners or deodorizers

Outdoors

- swimming pool
- pesticides
- toxic plants
- lawn fertilizers

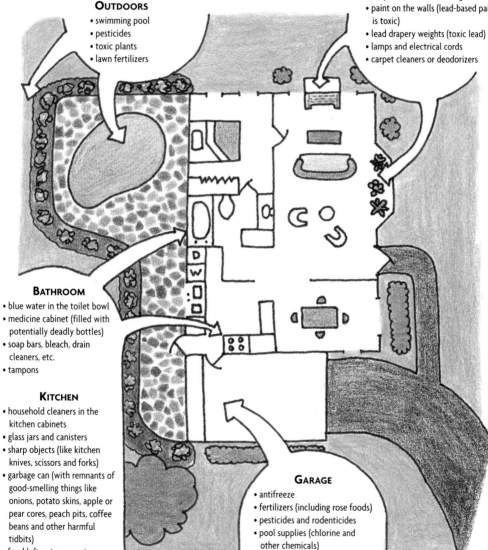

Bathroom

- blue water in the toilet bowl
- medicine cabinet (filled with potentially deadly bottles)
- soap bars, bleach, drain cleaners, etc.
- tampons

Kitchen

- household cleaners in the kitchen cabinets
- glass jars and canisters
- sharp objects (like kitchen knives, scissors and forks)
- garbage can (with remnants of good-smelling things like onions, potato skins, apple or pear cores, peach pits, coffee beans and other harmful tidbits)
- food left out on counters (some foods are toxic to dogs)

Garage

- antifreeze
- fertilizers (including rose foods)
- pesticides and rodenticides
- pool supplies (chlorine and other chemicals)
- oil and gasoline in containers
- sharp objects, electrical cords and power tools

The breeder introduces the young pup to a chew toy to encourage proper chewing behavior as he grows.

fertilizers, chemicals and tools are usually kept there. It's best to keep these areas off-limits to the dog. Antifreeze is especially dangerous to dogs, as they find the taste appealing and it takes only a few licks from the driveway to kill a dog, puppy or adult, small breed or large.

VISITING THE VETERINARIAN

A good veterinarian is your Norwich Terrier puppy's best health-insurance policy. If you do not already have a vet, ask your breeder, friends and experienced dog people in your area for recommendations so that you can select a vet before you bring your Norwich Terrier puppy home. Also arrange for your puppy's first veterinary examination beforehand, since many vets do not have appointments available immediately and your puppy should visit the veterinarian within a day or so of coming home.

It's important to make sure that your puppy's first visit to the vet is a pleasant and positive one. The vet should take great care to befriend the pup and handle him gently to make their first meeting a positive experience. The vet will give the pup a thorough physical examination and set up a schedule for vaccinations and other necessary wellness visits. Be sure to show your vet any health and inoculation records, which you should have received from your breeder. Your vet is a great source of canine health information, so be sure to ask questions and take notes. Creating a health journal for your puppy will make

ASK THE VET

Help your vet help you to become a well-informed dog owner. Don't be shy about becoming involved in your puppy's veterinary care by asking questions and gaining as much knowledge as you can. For starters, ask what shots your puppy is getting and what diseases they prevent, and discuss with your vet the safest way to vaccinate. Find out what is involved in your dog's annual wellness visits. If you plan to spay or neuter, discuss the best age at which to have this done. Start out on the right "paw" with your puppy's vet and develop good communication with him, as he will care for your dog's health throughout the dog's entire life.

a handy reference for his wellness and any future health problems that may arise.

MEETING THE FAMILY

Your Norwich Terrier's homecoming is an exciting time for all members of the family, and it's only natural that everyone will be eager to meet him, pet him and play with him. However, for the puppy's sake, it's best to make these initial family meetings as uneventful as possible so that the pup is not overwhelmed with too much too soon. Remember, he has just left his dam and his littermates and is away from the breeder's home for the first time. Despite his fuzzy wagging tail, he is still apprehensive and wondering where he is and who all these strange humans are. It's best to let him explore on his own and meet the family members as he feels comfortable. Let him investigate all the new smells, sights and sounds at his own pace. Children should be especially careful to not get overly excited, use loud voices or hug the pup too tightly. Be calm, gentle and affectionate, and be ready to comfort him if he appears frightened or uneasy.

Be sure to show your puppy his new crate during this first day home. Toss a treat or two inside the crate; if he associates the crate with food, he will associate the crate with good things. If he is

PUPPY PARASITES

Parasites are nasty little critters that live in or on your dog or puppy. Most puppies are born with ascarid roundworms, which are acquired from dormant ascarids residing in the dam. Other parasites can be acquired through contact with infected fecal matter. Take a stool sample to your vet for testing. He will prescribe a safe wormer to treat any parasites found in your puppy's stool. Always have a fecal test performed at your puppy's annual veterinary exam.

comfortable with the crate, you can offer him his first meal inside it. Leave the door ajar so he can wander in and out as he chooses.

FIRST NIGHT IN HIS NEW HOME

So much has happened in your Norwich Terrier puppy's first day away from the breeder. He's had his first car ride to his new home. He's met his new human family and perhaps the other family pets. He has explored his new house and yard, at least those places where he is to be allowed during his first weeks at home. He may have visited his new veterinarian. He has eaten his first meal or two away from his dam and litter-mates. Surely that's enough to tire out an eight-week-old Norwich Terrier pup...or so you hope!

It's bedtime. During the day,

the pup investigated his crate, which is his new den and sleeping space, so it is not entirely strange to him. Line the crate with a soft towel or blanket that he can snuggle into and gently place him into the crate for the night. Some breeders send home a piece of bedding from where the pup slept with his littermates, and those familiar scents are a great comfort for the puppy on his first night without his siblings.

He will probably whine or cry. The puppy is objecting to the confinement and the fact that he is alone for the first time. This can be a stressful time for you as well as for the pup. It's important that you remain strong and don't let the puppy out of his crate to comfort him. He will fall asleep eventually. If you release him, the puppy will learn that crying means "out" and will continue that habit. You are laying the groundwork for future habits. Some breeders find that soft music can soothe a crying pup and help him get to sleep.

SOCIALIZING YOUR PUPPY
The first 20 weeks of your Norwich Terrier puppy's life are the most important of his entire lifetime. A properly socialized puppy will grow up to be a confident and stable adult who will be a pleasure to live with and a welcome addition to the neighborhood.

The importance of socializa-

> **CONFINEMENT**
> It is wise to keep your puppy confined to a small "puppy-proofed" area of the house for his first few weeks at home. Gate or block off a space near the door he will use for outdoor potty trips. Expandable baby gates are useful to create puppy's designated area. If he is allowed to roam through the entire house or even only several rooms, it will be more difficult to house-train him.

tion cannot be overemphasized. Research on canine behavior has proven that puppies who are not exposed to new sights, sounds, people and animals during their first 20 weeks of life will grow up to be timid and fearful, even aggressive, and unable to flourish outside of their familiar home environment.

Socializing your puppy is not difficult and, in fact, will be a fun time for you both. Lead training goes hand in hand with socialization, so your puppy will be learning how to walk on a lead at the same time that he's meeting the neighborhood. Because the Norwich Terrier is such a terrific breed, your puppy will enjoy being "the new kid on the block." Take him for short walks, to the park and to other dog-friendly places where he will encounter new people, especially children. Puppies automatically recognize

Your Norwich pup will miss mealtime, naptime and playtime with his littermates— before you bring him home, they've done everything together.

children as "little people" and are drawn to play with them. Just make sure that you supervise these meetings and that the children do not get too rough or encourage him to play too hard. An overzealous pup can often nip too hard, frightening the child and in turn making the puppy overly

WATCH THE WATER

To help your puppy sleep through the night without having to relieve himself, remove his water bowl after 7 p.m. Offer him a couple of ice cubes during the evening to quench his thirst. Never leave water in a puppy's crate, as this is inviting puddles of mishaps.

excited. A bad experience in puppyhood can impact a dog for life, so a pup that has a negative experience with a child may grow up to be shy or even aggressive around children.

Take your puppy along on your daily errands. Puppies are natural "people magnets," and most people who see your pup will want to pet him. All of these encounters will help to mold him into a confident adult dog. Likewise, you will soon feel like a confident, responsible dog owner, rightly proud of your handsome Norwich Terrier.

Be especially careful of your puppy's encounters and experiences during the eight-to-ten-week-old period, which is also called the "fear period." This is a serious imprinting period, and all contact during this time should be gentle and positive. A frightening or negative event could leave a permanent impression that could affect his future behavior if a similar situation arises.

Also make sure that your puppy has received his first and second rounds of vaccinations before you expose him to other dogs or bring him to places that other dogs may frequent. Avoid dog parks and other strange-dog areas until your vet assures you that your puppy is fully immunized and resistant to the diseases that can be passed between canines. Discuss socialization with your breeder, as some breeders recommend socializing the puppy even before he has received all of his inoculations, depending on how outgoing the puppy may be.

LEADER OF THE PUPPY'S PACK
Like other canines, your puppy needs an authority figure, someone he can look up to and regard as the leader of his "pack." His first pack leader was his dam, who taught him to be polite and not chew too hard on her ears or nip at her muzzle. He learned those same lessons from his littermates. If he played too rough, they cried in pain and stopped the game, which sent an important message

to the rowdy puppy.

As puppies play together, they are also struggling to determine who will be the boss. Being pack animals, dogs need someone to be in charge. If a litter of puppies remained together beyond puppyhood, one of the pups

Be prepared for a busy, curious little dog, who can be a bit vocal and maybe even an escape artist when there's something interesting on the other side of the fence.

would emerge as the strongest one, the one who calls the shots.

Once your puppy leaves the pack, he will look intuitively for a new leader. If he does not recognize you as that leader, he will try to assume that position for himself. Of course, it is hard to imagine your adorable Norwich Terrier puppy trying to be in charge when he is so small and seemingly helpless. You must remember that these are natural canine instincts. Do not cave in and allow your pup to get the upper "paw"!

The breeder has begun the socialization process by introducing the puppy to adults in his own kennel. You must continue with socialization once the puppy arrives at your home.

Just as socialization is so important during these first 20 weeks, so too is your puppy's early education. He was born without any bad habits. He does not know what is good or bad behavior. If he does things like nipping and digging, it's because he is having fun and doesn't know that humans consider these things as "bad." It's your job to teach him proper puppy manners, and this is the best time to accomplish that...before he has developed bad habits, since it is much more difficult to "unlearn" or correct unacceptable learned behavior than to teach good behavior from the start.

Make sure that all members of the family understand the importance of being consistent when training their new puppy. If you tell the puppy to stay off the sofa and your daughter allows him to cuddle on the couch to watch her favorite TV show with her, your pup will be confused about what he is and is not allowed to do. Have a family conference before your pup comes home so that everyone understands the basic principles of puppy training and the rules you have set forth for the pup, and agrees to follow them.

The old saying that "an ounce of prevention is worth a pound of cure" is especially true when it comes to puppies. It is much easier to prevent inappropriate behavior than it is to change it. It's also easier and less stressful for the pup, since it will keep discipline to a minimum and create a more positive learning environment for him. That, in turn, will also be easier on you!

Here are a few commonsense tips to keep your belongings safe and your puppy out of trouble:
• Keep your closet doors closed

TEETHING TIME

All puppies chew. It's normal canine behavior. Chewing just plain feels good to a puppy, especially during the three- to five-month teething period when the adult teeth are breaking through the gums. Rather than attempting to eliminate such a strong natural chewing instinct, you will be more successful if you redirect it and teach your puppy what he may or may not chew. Correct inappropriate chewing with a sharp "No!" and offer him a chew toy, praising him when he takes it. Don't become discouraged. Chewing usually decreases after the adult teeth have come in.

and your shoes, socks and other apparel off the floor so your puppy can't get at them.

- Keep a secure lid on the trash container or put the trash where your puppy can't dig into it. He can't damage what he can't reach!
- Supervise your puppy at all times to make sure he is not getting into mischief. If he starts to chew the corner of the rug, you can distract him instantly by tossing a toy for him to fetch. You also will be able to whisk him outside when you notice that he is about to piddle on the carpet. If you can't see your puppy, you can't teach him or correct his behavior.

SOLVING PUPPY PROBLEMS

Chewing and Nipping

Nipping at fingers and toes is normal puppy behavior. Chewing is also the way that puppies investigate their surroundings. However, you will have to teach your puppy that chewing anything other than his toys is not acceptable. That won't happen overnight and at times puppy teeth will test your patience. However, if you allow nipping and chewing to continue, just think about the damage that a mature Norwich can do with a full set of adult terrier teeth.

Whenever your puppy nips your hand or fingers, cry out "Ouch!" in a loud voice, which should startle your puppy and stop him from nipping, even if only for a moment. Immediately

Here's a unique socialization experience for the Norwich. Dogs raised on farms will meet lots of other two- and four-footed creatures that urban dogs can only dream about.

distract him by offering a small treat or an appropriate toy for him to chew instead (which means having chew toys and puppy treats handy or in your pockets at all times). Praise him when he takes the toy and tell him what a good fellow he is. Praise is just as or even more important in puppy training as discipline and correction—positive reinforcement is the way to go.

Puppies also tend to nip at children more often than adults, since they perceive little ones to be more vulnerable and more similar to their littermates. Teach your children appropriate responses to nipping behavior. If they are unable to handle it

themselves, you may have to intervene. Puppy nips can be quite painful and a child's frightened reaction will only encourage a puppy to nip harder, which is a natural canine response. As with all other puppy situations, interaction between your Norwich Terrier puppy and children should be supervised.

Chewing on objects, not just family members' fingers and ankles, is also normal canine behavior that can be especially tedious (for the owner, not the pup) during the teething period when the puppy's adult teeth are coming in. At this stage, chewing just plain feels good. Furniture legs and cabinet corners are common puppy favorites. Shoes and other personal items also taste pretty good to a pup.

The best solution is, once again, prevention. If you value something, keep it tucked away and out of reach. You can't hide your dining-room table in a closet, but you can try to deflect the chewing by applying a bitter product made just to deter dogs from chewing. Available in a spray or cream, this substance is vile-tasting, although safe for dogs, and most puppies will avoid the forbidden object after one tiny taste. You also can apply the product to your leather leash if the puppy tries to chew on his lead during leash-training sessions.

Despite their size difference, these Norwich and Standard Poodle buddies have a lot in common—both breeds are robust, agile and intelligent and make alert watchdogs.

Norwich Terriers share part of their history with horses, as sometimes the small terriers were brought along by hunters on horseback. Today some farm Norwich still share their lives with equine friends.

Keep a ready supply of safe chews handy to offer your Norwich Terrier as a distraction when he starts to chew on something that's a "no-no." Remember, at this tender age he does not yet know what is permitted or forbidden, so you have to be "on call" every minute he's awake and on the prowl.

You may lose a treasure or two during puppy's growing-up period, and the furniture could sustain a nasty nick or two. These can be trying times, so be prepared for those inevitable accidents and comfort yourself in knowing that this too shall pass.

PUPPY WHINING
Puppies often cry and whine, just as infants and little children do. It's their way of telling us that they are lonely or in need of attention. Your puppy will miss his littermates and will feel insecure when he is left alone. You may be out of the house or just in another room, but he will still feel alone. During these times, the puppy's crate should be his personal comfort station, a

the sound of human voices can be soothing and will give the impression that people are around.

Give your puppy a favorite cuddly toy or chew toy to entertain him whenever he is crated. You will both be happier: the puppy because he is safe in his den and you because he is quiet, safe and not getting into puppy escapades that can wreak havoc in your house or cause him danger.

To make sure that your puppy will always view his crate as a safe and cozy place, never, *ever*, use the crate as punishment. That's the best way to turn the crate into a negative place that the pup will want to avoid. Sure, you can use the crate for your own peace of mind if your puppy is getting into trouble and needs some "time out." Just don't let him know that! Never scold the pup and immediately place him into the crate. Count to ten, give him a couple of hugs and maybe a treat, then scoot him into his crate.

It's also important not to make a big fuss when he is released from the crate. That will make getting out of the crate more appealing than being in the crate, which is just the opposite of what you are trying to achieve.

Domestic Squabbles
How well your new Norwich Terrier will get along with an

Norwich Terriers approach all they do with a joy for life that's quite contagious! place all his own where he can feel safe and secure. Once he learns that being alone is okay and not something to be feared, he will settle down without crying or objecting. You might want to leave a radio on while he is crated, as

THE FAMILY FELINE

A resident cat has feline squatter's rights. The cat will treat the newcomer (your puppy) as she sees fit, regardless of what you do or say. So it's best to let the two of them work things out on their own terms. Cats have a height advantage and will generally leap to higher ground to avoid direct contact with a rambunctious pup. Some will hiss and boldly swat at a pup who passes by or tries to reach the cat. Keep the puppy under control in the presence of the cat and they will eventually become accustomed to each other.

Here's a hint: move the cat's litter box where the puppy can't get into it! It's best to do so well before the pup comes home so the cat is used to the new location.

older dog who has squatter's rights depends largely on the individual dogs. Like people, some dogs are more gregarious than others and will enjoy having a furry friend to play with. Others will not be thrilled at the prospect of sharing their dog space with a canine newcomer.

It's best to introduce the dogs to each other on neutral ground, away from home, so the resident dog won't feel so possessive. Keep both puppy and adult on loose leads (loose is very important, as a tight lead sends negative signals and can intimi-date either dog) and allow them to sniff and do their doggy things. A few raised hackles are normal, with the older dog pawing at the youngster. Let the two work things out between them unless you see signs of real aggression, such as deep growls or curled lips and serious snarls. You may have to keep them separated until the veteran gets used to the new family member, often after the pup has outgrown the silly puppy stage and is more mature in stature. Take precautions to make sure that the puppy does not become frightened by the older dog's behavior.

Whatever happens, it's important to make your resident dog feel secure. (Jealousy is normal among dogs, too!) Pay extra attention to the older dog: feed him first, hug him first and don't insist he share his toys or space with the new pup until he's ready. If the two are still at odds months later, consult an obedience professional for advice.

Cat introductions are easier, believe it or not. Being agile and independent creatures, cats will scoot to high places, out of the puppy's reach. A cat might even tease the puppy and cuff him from above when the pup comes within paw's reach. However, most will end up buddies if you just let dog-and-cat nature run its course.

NORWICH TERRIER

FEEDING YOUR NORWICH TERRIER

When you first take your Norwich puppy home, the breeder will encourage you to continue feeding the dog what he has been fed up to then. Any changes to his diet should be made gradually to avoid upsetting the puppy's digestion. Up to about four months of age, your Norwich will need about four meals a day. Feedings can then be reduced to three, and then to twice daily at around eight months of age. Adult Norwich normally thrive on one meal a day, with a few good, hard biscuits every day to help keep his teeth clean.

Be cautious about giving milk to your Norwich puppy.

Pups are introduced to solid food as part of the weaning process.

Avoid cow's milk, choosing instead dried milk made especially for dogs. Also, be wary of allergies to milk. Some Norwich cannot tolerate dairy products—which is not really a problem, since your adult dog will not require milk.

With today's variety of nutritionally complete foods, choosing what you feed your Norwich should depend on what keeps your dog fit and what works best for you. Balance is the key and a good manufactured dog food should include proteins, carbohydrates, vitamins and minerals. If you choose to incorporate some fresh foods into his diet, the Norwich is a natural meat eater, but will be happy to vary his diet with fish, eggs and cheese. Fresh foods should be chosen to not upset the balanced nutrition in good complete dog food.

While most Norwich have healthy appetites, you may find yourself with a finicky eater and a little resourcefulness on your part will be required. Patient trial and error to find what he likes will usually solve the dilemma, as well as trying feedings at different times.

Some Norwich breeders encourage owners to supplement their dogs' diets with vitamin B. Brewer's yeast tablets, a good source of vitamin B, are easily available, and breeders find this supplement quite beneficial for the breed. Vitamin E is also recommended for keeping the coat in good, healthy, shiny condition. Always consult your vet before giving any vitamin supplementation.

FEEDING THE PUPPY

Of course, your pup's very first food will be his dam's milk. There may be special situations in which pups fail to nurse, necessitating that the breeder hand-feed them with a formula, but, for the most part, pups spend the first weeks of life nursing from their dam. The breeder weans the pups by gradually introducing solid foods and decreasing the milk meals. Pups may even start themselves off on the weaning process, albeit inadvertently, if they snatch bites from their mom's food bowl.

By the time the pups are ready for new homes, they are fully weaned and eating a good puppy food. As a new owner, you may be thinking, "Great! The breeder has taken care of the hard part." Not so fast.

TEST FOR PROPER DIET
A good test for proper diet is the color, odor and firmness of your dog's stool. A healthy dog usually produces two or three semi-hard stools per day. The stools should have no unpleasant odor. They should be the same color from excretion to excretion.

A puppy's first year of life is the time when all or most of his growth and development takes place. This is a delicate time, and diet plays a huge role in proper skeletal and muscular formation. Improper diet and exercise habits can lead to damaging problems that will compromise the dog's health and movement for his entire life. That being said, new owners should not worry needlessly. With the myriad types of food formulated specifically for growing pups of different-sized breeds, dog-food manufacturers have taken much of the guesswork out of feeding your puppy well. Since growth-food formulas are designed to provide the nutrition that a growing puppy needs, it is unnecessary and, in fact, can prove harmful to add supplements to the diet. Research has shown that too much of certain vitamin supplements and minerals predispose a dog to skeletal problems. It's by no means a case of "if a little is good, a lot is better." At every stage of your dog's life, too much or too little in the way of nutrients can be harmful, which is why a manufactured complete food is the easiest way to know that your dog is getting what he needs.

Because of a young pup's small body and accordingly small digestive system, his daily portion will be divided up into small meals throughout the day, with the number of feedings

This Norwich pup is truly getting into his meal!

> ### NOT HUNGRY?
> No dog in his right mind would turn down his dinner, would he? If you notice that your dog has lost interest in his food, there could be any number of causes. Dental problems are a common cause of appetite loss, one that is often overlooked. If your dog has a toothache, a loose tooth or sore gums from infection, chances are it doesn't feel so good to chew. Think about when you've had a toothache! If your dog does not approach the food bowl with his usual enthusiasm, look inside his mouth for signs of a problem. Whatever the cause, you'll want to consult your vet so that your chow hound can get back to his happy, hungry self as soon as possible.

decreased as mentioned as the puppy grows. Regarding the feeding schedule, feeding the pup at the same times and in the same place each day is important for both house-breaking purposes and establishing the dog's everyday routine. As for the amount to feed, growing puppies generally need proportionately more food per body weight than their adult counterparts, but a pup should never be allowed to gain excess weight. Dogs of all ages should be kept in proper body condition, but extra weight can strain a pup's developing frame, causing skeletal problems.

Watch your pup's weight as he grows and, if the recommended amounts seem to be too much or too little for your pup, consult the vet about appropriate dietary changes. Keep in mind that treats, although small, can quickly add up throughout the day,

Norwich typically have good appetites and look forward to mealtimes.

DIET DON'TS

- Got milk? Don't give it to your dog! Dogs cannot tolerate large quantities of cows' milk, as they do not have the enzymes to digest lactose.
- You may have heard of dog owners who add raw eggs to their dogs' food for a shiny coat or to make the food more palatable, but consumption of raw eggs too often can cause a deficiency of the vitamin biotin.
- Avoid feeding table scraps, as they will upset the balance of the dog's complete food. Additionally, fatty or highly seasoned foods can cause upset canine stomachs.
- Do not offer raw meat to your dog. Raw meat can contain parasites; it also is high in fat.
- Vitamin A toxicity in dogs can be caused by too much raw liver, especially if the dog already gets enough vitamin A in his balanced diet, which should be the case.
- Bones like chicken, pork chop and other soft bones are not suitable, as they easily splinter.

contributing unnecessary calories. Treats are fine when used prudently; opt for dog treats specially formulated to be healthy or for nutritious snacks like small pieces of cheese or cooked chicken.

FEEDING THE ADULT DOG

For the adult (meaning physically mature) dog, feeding properly is about maintenance, not growth. Again, correct weight is a concern. Your dog should appear fit and should have an evident "waist." His ribs should not be protruding (a sign of being underweight), but they should be covered by only a slight layer of fat. Under normal circumstances, an adult dog can be maintained fairly easily with a high-quality nutritionally complete adult-formula food.

Factor treats into your dog's overall daily caloric intake, and avoid offering table scraps. Not only are certain "people foods," including chocolate, onions, nuts, grapes and raisins, toxic to dogs, but feeding from the table encourages begging and overeating. Overweight dogs are more prone to health problems. Research has even shown that obesity takes years off a dog's life. With that in mind, resist the urge to overfeed and over-treat.

A Norwich won't turn down a tasty morsel! Don't make unnecessary additions to your dog's diet, whether with tidbits or with extra vitamins and minerals.

The amount of food needed for proper maintenance will vary depending on the individual dog's activity level, but you will be able to tell whether the daily portions are keeping him in good shape. With the wide variety of good complete foods available, choosing what to feed is largely a matter of personal preference. Just as with the puppy, the adult dog should have consistency in his

There is simply no better diet than mother's milk for the first weeks of a Norwich's life.

mealtimes and feeding place. In addition to a consistent routine, regular mealtimes also allow the owner to see how much his dog is eating. If the dog seems never to be satisfied or, likewise, becomes uninterested in his food, the owner will know right away that something is wrong and can consult the vet.

DIETS FOR THE AGING DOG

A good rule of thumb is that once a dog has reached 75% of his expected lifespan, he has reached "senior citizen" or geriatric status. Your Norwich Terrier will be considered a senior at about 9 years of age; based on his size, he has a projected lifespan of about 12–15 years. (The smallest breeds generally enjoy the longest lives and the largest breeds the shortest.)

What does aging have to do with your dog's diet? No, he won't get a discount at the local diner's early-bird special. Yes, he will require some dietary changes to accommodate the changes that come along with increased age. One change is that the older dog's dietary needs become more similar to that of a puppy. Specifically, dogs can metabolize more protein as youngsters and seniors than in the adult-maintenance stage. Discuss with your vet whether you need to switch to a higher-protein or senior-formulated food or whether your current adult-dog food contains sufficient nutrition for the senior.

Watching the dog's weight remains essential, even more so in the senior stage. Older dogs are already more vulnerable to illness, and obesity only contributes to their susceptibility to problems. As the older dog becomes less active and, thus, exercises less, his regular portions may cause him to gain weight. At this point, you may consider decreasing his daily food intake or switching to a reduced-calorie food. As with other changes, you should consult your vet for advice.

DON'T FORGET THE WATER!

For a dog, it's always time for a drink! Regardless of what type of food he eats, there's no doubt that he needs plenty of water. Fresh cold water, in a clean bowl, should be freely available to your dog at all times. There are special circumstances, such as during puppy housebreaking, when you will want to monitor your pup's water intake so that you will be able to predict when he will need to relieve himself, but water must be available to him nonetheless. Water is essential for hydration and proper body function just as it is in humans.

A good complete dry food should maintain your adult Norwich in fit condition.

You will get to know how much your dog typically drinks in a day. Of course, in the heat or if exercising vigorously, he will be more thirsty and will drink more. However, if he begins to drink noticeably more water for no apparent reason, this could signal any of various problems, and you are advised to consult your vet.

Water is the best drink for dogs. Some owners are tempted to give milk from time to time or to moisten dry food with milk, but dogs do not have the enzymes necessary to digest the lactose in milk, which is much different from the milk that nursing puppies receive. Therefore, stick with clean fresh water to quench your dog's thirst, and always have it readily available to him.

EXERCISE AND ACTIVITIES

While the Norwich Terrier will proudly catch a rat or bolt a fox for you, today he is primarily a companion dog and will be equally as happy to stroll around the yard or neighborhood with his family. Still, he is an active, hardy little fellow and you will bring out his best with a sufficient amount of exercise.

If you live in the country, your Norwich will dazzle you with his curiosity and stamina. He will love the opportunity to race about and explore, but you should provide him with a large enclosed area for his exercise or keep him on a long lead that allows him plenty of room to roam. He will be off and running at the sight of any perceived "prey," so you must keep him safe. And, as with any dog outdoors, do make sure he has an identification tag.

The Norwich in the suburbs

PUPPY STEPS

Puppies are brimming with activity and enthusiasm. It seems that they can play all day and night without tiring, but don't overdo your puppy's exercise regimen. Easy does it for the puppy's first six to nine months. Keep walks brief and don't let the puppy engage in stressful jumping games. The puppy frame is delicate, and too much exercise during those critical growing months can cause injury to his bone structure, ligaments and musculature. Save his first jog for his first birthday!

WEIGHT AND SEE!

When you look at yourself in the mirror each day, you get very used to what you see! It's only when you pull out last year's vacation outfit and can't zip it up that you notice that you've put on some pounds. Dog owners are the same way with their dogs. Often a few pounds go unnoticed, and it's not until some time passes or the vet remarks that your dog looks more than pleasantly plump that you realize what's happened. To avoid your pet's becoming obese right under your very nose, make a habit of routinely evaluating his condition with a hands-on test.

Can you feel, but not see, your dog's rib cage? Does your dog have a waist? His waist should be evident by touch and also visible from above and from the side. In top view, the dog's body should have an hourglass shape. These are indicators of good condition.

While it's not hard to spot an extremely skinny or overly rotund dog, it's the subtle changes that lead up to under- or overweight condition of which we must be aware. If your dog's ribs are visible, he is too thin. Conversely, if you can't feel the ribs under too much fat, and if there's no indication of a waistline, your dog is overweight. Both of these conditions require changes to the diet. A trip or sometimes just a call to the vet will help you modify your dog's feeding.

should not be allowed to laze around without any exercise. Just being outdoors in a fenced yard does not compensate for a couple of good walks each day on lead. A nice walk through the neighborhood will stimulate his terrier inquisitiveness and keep him happy and fit. At least half an hour of daily exercise is good for the Norwich and, of course, his favorite activities will be things done with you.

The same should be encouraged for the city dweller. The Norwich thrives on regular walks, and, whether on city sidewalks or in parks, he will love these opportunities to explore and socialize. If your neighborhood has a dog run or park, where he is safe from escape and injury, do let him off lead to enjoy a good scamper and scramble.

A doggie door gives your Norwich Terrier access to the fenced yard as he pleases. This type of device can be quite convenient for the busy dog owner, and some new models even have security features so that only your dog can get in.

For those with the interest and energy, there are almost always weekend tracking and earthdog trials, scent hurdle races and obedience and agility competitions. You and your Norwich both will be well exercised after these events! The Norwich Terrier is, above all, adaptable. He wants nothing more than to be by your side, but he won't say "no" to a good romp. Exercise will keep a Norwich fit, happily occupied and less prone to destructive behavior caused by boredom, and thus a more rewarding companion.

GROOMING YOUR NORWICH TERRIER
While most terrier breeds are clipped, snipped and trimmed to perfection, the Norwich Terrier is said to be one of the easiest of the terriers to groom. His preferred look is natural, meaning not clipped or sculpted, which makes him ideal for those who want a "wash-and-wear" companion. Indeed, this is not a trimmed breed. Unless you plan to show your Norwich, this double-coated dog—hard, wiry outer "jacket" covering a softer undercoat—responds best to basic brushing and some hand-stripping to pluck out the dead hairs.

A simple daily brushing to avoid knots and tangles is recommended, though a thorough grooming once a week will keep your Norwich in prime condition. It will also give you the opportunity to examine your dog for any ear, eye or skin problems. Many dogs look forward to their grooming routine. If you accustom your Norwich to being brushed and handled, he will come to see the experience as enjoyable, an opportunity to spend time with you. If your dog seems a bit hesitant or feisty at first, try alternating a little massage along with the brushing, or give him an occasional treat as you groom.

Within our human family, keeping a youngster clean and healthy expresses our love and concern for the child. It is the same for your dog. Your Norwich will appreciate the care you show him and see the experience as an expression of your love. Don't be surprised if he soon races over to you when you get out his brush!

The tools you need are simple and easy to use. Practice makes perfect, and in no time at all you will be doing a good job. Start with a rubber-backed wire pin brush. This brush, used by professional Norwich handlers, cleans and grooms the coat without tearing out the soft undercoat. A terrier comb with teeth not too closely spaced will, likewise, help take out the tangles without pulling and cutting the coat. Generally, a fine comb is used mainly for the ears and around the face, and the coarse comb is a good tool for stripping the body coat.

Using the wire brush, start at the head and face, gently brushing out each hair and then going down the front, ruff and sides of the shoulders. Then move on to under his body, holding the dog up to carefully brush his tummy and the underside of each front leg. After you've done his front, you can turn the dog with his rear to you and brush down from his neck to his tail, brushing along the sides as you move back and down. Then go down each back leg, in between the legs and, finally, brush the tail. This thorough brushing will loosen and encourage loss of any dead body hair.

Afterwards you can take the comb over the body and work out any small knots encountered. All of this should be done most gently. Your Norwich will be particularly sensitive in between the legs and around his muzzle. A good brushing stimulates the hair roots and gives a nice rich look to the furnishings.

Once or twice a year, the coat of your Norwich will be full-blown (ready to shed), and

A wire pin brush is useful on the Norwich Terrier's outer coat.

Use a steel comb around the neck and on the furnishings to keep them tangle-free.

The eye area is kept clean easily with a soft wipe and cleaning solution made for this purpose.

WATER SHORTAGE

No matter how well behaved your dog is, bathing is always a project! Nothing can substitute for a good warm bath, but owners do have the option of giving their dogs "dry" baths. Pet shops sell excellent products, in both powder and spray forms, designed for spot-cleaning your dog. These dry shampoos are convenient for touch-up jobs when you don't have the time to bathe your dog in the traditional way.

Muddy feet, messy behinds and smelly coats can be spot-cleaned and deodorized with a "wet-nap"-style cleaner. On those days when your dog insists on rolling in fresh goose droppings and there's no time for a bath, a spot bath can save the day. These pre-moistened wipes are also handy for other grooming needs like wiping faces, ears and eyes and freshening tails and behinds.

strip it (pluck it) out with your finger and thumb. You can do this a little every day as part of your terrier's grooming routine. If your breeder is nearby, you may find that he will be happy to strip your dog for you.

Some call the Norwich a "self-cleaning" dog. His weather-resistant coat sheds dirt and has no odor. Good nutrition and a simple grooming routine will keep his coat healthy and smart-looking.

BATHING

In general, dogs need to be bathed only a few times a year, possibly more often if your dog gets into something messy or if he decides to dig a trench. Show dogs are usually bathed before every show, which could be as frequent as weekly, although this depends on the owner. Bathing too frequently can have negative effects on the skin and coat, removing natural oils, causing dryness and altering the harsh texture.

If you give your dog his first bath when he is young, he will become accustomed to the process. Wrestling a dog into the tub or chasing a freshly shampooed dog who has escaped from the bath will be no fun! Most dogs don't naturally enjoy their baths, but you at least want yours to cooperate with you.

Before bathing the dog, have the items you'll need close at hand. First decide where you will

it should be stripped to the undercoat to allow room for more hair growth. While the show Norwich requires a more artful hand, the pet Norwich will look good with some basic "tidying." If you take your dog to a profes-sional groomer, do ask them to hand-strip, as clippers can make the coat too soft, which is unchar-acteristic for our breed. If you prefer to do it yourself, you will find it is not all that difficult. Wait until the hair is really dead and

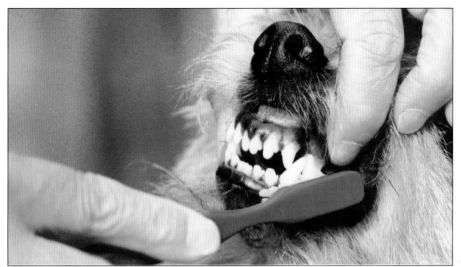

Yes, we brush our dogs' teeth! Specially made doggy tooth-brushes and paste are available from your vet or pet-supply store. This is an essential part of your Norwich's home-care routine.

bathe the dog. You should have a tub or basin with a non-slip surface. Puppies can even be bathed in a sink. In warm weather, some like to use a portable pool in the yard, although you'll want to make sure your dog doesn't head for the nearest dirt pile following his bath! You will also need a hose or shower spray to wet the coat thoroughly, a shampoo formulated for dogs, absorbent towels and perhaps a blow dryer. Human shampoos are too harsh for dogs' coats and will dry them out.

Before wetting the dog, give him a brush-through to remove any dead hair, dirt and mats. Make sure he is at ease in the tub and have the water at a comfortable temperature. Begin bathing by wetting the coat all the way down to the skin. Massage in the shampoo, keeping it away from

his face and eyes. Rinse him thoroughly, again avoiding the eyes and ears, as you don't want to get water into the ear canals. A thorough rinsing is important, as shampoo residue is drying and itchy to the dog. After rinsing, wrap him in a towel to absorb the initial moisture. You can finish drying with either a towel or a blow dryer on low heat, held at a safe distance from the dog. You should keep the dog indoors and away from drafts until he is completely dry.

NAIL CLIPPING

Having his nails trimmed is not on many dogs' lists of favorite things to do. With this in mind, you will need to accustom your puppy to the procedure at a young age so that he will sit still (well, as still as he can) for his pedicures. Long

SCOOTING HIS BOTTOM

Here's a doggy problem that many owners tend to neglect. If your dog is scooting his rear end around the carpet, he probably is experiencing anal-sac impaction or blockage. The anal sacs are the two grape-sized glands on either side of the dog's vent. The dog cannot empty these glands, which become filled with a foul-smelling material. The dog may attempt to lick the area to relieve the pressure. He may also rub his anus on your walls, furniture or floors.

Don't neglect your dog's rear end during grooming sessions. By squeezing both sides of the anus with a soft cloth, you can express some of the material in the sacs. If the material is pasty and thick, you likely will need the assistance of a veterinarian. Vets know how to express the glands and can show you how to do it correctly without hurting the dog or spraying yourself with the unpleasant liquid.

nails can cause the dog's feet to spread, which is not good for him; likewise, long nails can hurt if they unintentionally scratch, not good for you!

Some dogs' nails are worn down naturally by regular walking on hard surfaces, so the frequency with which you clip depends on your individual dog. Look at his nails from time to time and clip as needed; a good way to know when it's time for a trim is if you hear your dog clicking as he walks across the floor.

There are several types of nail clippers and even electric nail-grinding tools made for dogs; first we'll discuss using the clipper. To start, have your clipper ready and some doggie treats on hand. You want your pup to view his nail-clipping sessions in a positive light, and what better way to convince him than with food? You may want to enlist the help of an assistant to comfort the pup and offer treats as you concentrate on the clipping itself. The guillotine-type clipper is thought of by many as the easiest type to use; the nail tip is inserted into the opening, and blades on the top and bottom snip it off in one clip.

Start by grasping the pup's paw; a little pressure on the foot pad causes the nail to extend, making it easier to clip. Clip off a little at a time. If you can see the "quick," which is a blood vessel that runs through each nail, you will know how much to trim, as you do not want to cut into the quick. On that note, if you do cut the quick, which will cause bleeding, you can stem the flow of blood with a styptic pencil or other clotting agent. If you mistakenly nip the quick, do not panic or fuss, as this will cause the pup to be afraid. Simply reassure the pup, stop the bleeding and move on to the next nail. Don't be discouraged; you will become a professional canine pedicurist with practice.

You may or may not be able to see the quick, so it's best to just clip off a small bit at a time. If you see a dark dot in the center of the nail, this is the quick and your cue to stop clipping. Tell the puppy he's a "good boy" and offer a piece of treat with each nail. You can also use nail-clipping time to examine the footpads, making sure that they are not dry and cracked and that nothing has become embedded in them.

The nail grinder, the other choice, is many owners' first choice. Accustoming the puppy to the sound of the grinder and sensation of the buzz presents fewer challenges than the clipper, and there's no chance of cutting through the quick. Use the grinder on a low setting and always talk soothingly to your dog. He won't mind his salon visit, and he'll have nicely polished nails as well.

EYE CARE

During grooming sessions, pay extra attention to the condition of your dog's eyes. If the area around the eyes is soiled or if tear staining has occurred, there are various cleaning agents made especially for this purpose. Look at the dog's eyes to make sure no debris has entered; dogs with large eyes and those who spend time outdoors are especially prone to this.

The signs of an eye infection are obvious: mucus, redness, puffiness, scabs or other signs of irritation. If your dog's eyes become infected, the vet will likely prescribe an antibiotic ointment for treatment. If you notice signs of more serious problems, such as opacities in the eye, which usually indicate cataracts, consult the vet at once.

THE EARS KNOW

Examining and cleaning your puppy's ears helps ensure good internal health. The ears are the eyes to the dog's innards! Begin handling your puppy's ears when he's still young so that he doesn't protest every time you lift a flap or touch his ears. Yeast and bacteria are two of the culprits that you can detect by examining the ear. You will notice a strong, often foul, odor, debris, redness or some kind of discharge. All of these point to health problems that can worsen over time. Additionally, you are on the lookout for wax accumulation, ear mites and other tiny bothersome parasites and their even tinier droppings. You may have to pluck hair with tweezers in order to have a better view into the dog's ears, but this is painless if done carefully. Healthy ears should be cleaned weekly with an ear-cleaning powder or liquid carefully applied with a cotton ball or pad. Never probe into the dog's ear canal; cotton swabs can be dangerous.

Taking time to pay attention to your dog's eyes will alert you in the early stages of any problem so that you can get your dog treatment as soon as possible. You could save your dog's sight!

ID FOR YOUR DOG

You love your Norwich Terrier and want to keep him safe. Of course, you take every precaution to prevent his escaping from the yard or becoming lost or stolen. You have a sturdy high fence and you always keep your dog on lead when out and about in public places. If your dog is not properly identified, however, you are overlooking a major aspect of his safety. We hope to never be in a situation where our dog is missing, but we should practice prevention in the unfortunate case that this happens; identification greatly increases the chances of your dog's being returned to you

There are several ways to identify your dog. First, the traditional dog tag should be a staple in your dog's wardrobe, attached to his everyday collar. Tags can be made of sturdy plastic and various metals and should include your contact information so that a person who finds the dog can get in touch with you right away to arrange his return. Many people today enjoy the wide range of decorative tags available, so have fun and create a tag to match your dog's personality. Of course,

---

PET OR STRAY?

Besides the obvious benefit of providing your contact information to whoever finds your lost dog, an ID tag makes your dog more approachable and more likely to be recovered. A strange dog wandering the neighborhood without a collar and tags will look like a stray, while the collar and tags indicate that the dog is someone's pet. Even if the ID tags become detached from the collar, the collar alone will make a person more likely to pick up the dog.

---

it is important that the tag stays on the collar, so have a secure "O" ring attachment; you also can explore the type of tag that slides right onto the collar.

In addition to the ID tag, which every dog should wear even if identified by another method, two other forms of identification have become popular: microchipping and tattooing. In microchipping, a tiny scannable chip is painlessly inserted under the dog's skin. The number is registered to you so that, if your lost dog turns up at a clinic or shelter, the chip can be scanned to retrieve your contact information.

The advantage of the microchip is that it is a permanent form of ID, but there are some factors to consider. Several different companies make microchips, and not all are compatible with the others' scanning devices. It's best to find a company with a universal microchip that can be read by scanners made by other companies as well. It won't do any good to have the dog chipped if the information cannot be retrieved. Also, not every humane society, shelter and clinic is equipped with a scanner, although more and more facilities are equipping themselves. In fact, many shelters microchip dogs that they adopt out to new homes.

In the US, there are five or six major microchip manufacturers as well as a few databases. The American Kennel Club's Companion Animal Recovery unit works in conjunction with HomeAgain™ Companion Animal Retrieval System (Schering-Plough). In the UK, The Kennel Club is affiliated with the National Pet Register, operated by Wood Green Animal Shelters.

Because the microchip is not visible to the eye, the dog must wear a tag that states that he is microchipped so that whoever picks him up will know to have him scanned. He of course also should have a tag with contact information in case his chip cannot be read. Humane societies and veterinary clinics offer microchipping service, which is usually very affordable.

Though less popular than microchipping, tattooing is another permanent method of ID for dogs. Most vets perform this service, and there are also clinics that perform dog tattooing. This is also an affordable procedure and one that will not cause much discomfort for the dog. It is best to put the tattoo in a visible area, such as the ear, to deter theft. It is sad to say that there are cases of dogs' being stolen and sold to research laboratories, but such laboratories will not accept tattooed dogs.

To ensure that the tattoo is effective in aiding your dog's return to you, the tattoo number must be registered with a national organization. That way, when someone finds a tattooed dog, a phone call to the registry will quickly match the dog with his owner.

CAR CAUTION

You may like to bring your canine companion along on the daily errands, but if you will be running in and out from place to place and can't bring him indoors with you, leave him at home. Your dog should never be left alone in the car, not even for a minute—never! A car heats up very quickly, and even a cracked-open window will not help. In fact, leaving the window cracked will be dangerous if the dog becomes uncomfortable and tries to escape, and may even attract a dog thief. When in doubt, leave your dog home, where you know he will be safe.

NORWICH TERRIER

BASIC TRAINING PRINCIPLES: PUPPY VS. ADULT

There's a big difference between training an adult dog and training a young puppy. With a young puppy, everything is new. At eight to ten weeks of age, he will be experiencing many things, and he has nothing with which to compare these experiences. Up to this point, he has been with his dam and littermates, not one-on-one with people except in his

Training unlocks not just good manners but also the world of potential in this bright, athletic, versatile terrier.

interactions with his breeder and visitors to the litter.

When you first bring the puppy home, he is eager to please you. This means that he accepts doing things your way. During the next couple of months, he will absorb the basis of everything he needs to know for the rest of his life. This early age is even referred to as the "sponge" stage. After that, for the next 18 months, it's up to you to reinforce good manners by building on the foundation that you've established. Once your puppy is reliable in basic commands and behavior and has reached the appropriate age, you may gradually introduce him to some of the interesting sports, games and activities available to pet owners and their dogs.

Raising your puppy is a family affair. Each member of the family must know what rules to set forth for the puppy and how to use the same one-word commands to mean exactly the same thing every time. Even if yours is a large family, one person will soon be considered by the pup to be the leader, the Alpha person in his pack, the "boss" who must be obeyed. Often that highly regarded person turns out to be the one who feeds the puppy. Food ranks very high on the puppy's list of important things! That's why your puppy is rewarded with small treats along with verbal praise when he responds to you correctly. As the puppy learns to do what you want him to do, the food rewards are gradually eliminated and only the praise remains. If you were to keep up with the food treats, you could have two problems on your hands—an obese dog and a beggar.

Training begins the minute your Norwich Terrier puppy steps through the doorway of your home, so don't make the mistake of putting the puppy on the floor and telling him by your actions to "Go for it! Run wild!" Even if this is your first puppy, you must act as if you know what you're doing: be the boss. An uncertain pup may be terrified to move, while a bold one will be ready to take you at your word and start plotting to destroy the house! Before you collected your puppy, you decided where his own special place would be, and that's where to put him when you first arrive home. Give him a house tour after he has investigated his area and had a nap and a bathroom "pit stop."

It's worth mentioning here that, if you've adopted an adult dog that is completely trained to

> ### I WILL FOLLOW YOU
> Obedience isn't just a classroom activity. In your home you have many great opportunities to teach your dog polite manners. Allowing your pet on the bed or furniture elevates him to your level, which is not a good idea (the word is "Off!"). Use the "umbilical cord" method, keeping your dog on lead so he has to go with you wherever you go. You sit, he sits. You walk, he heels. You stop, he sit-stays. Everywhere you go, he's with you, but you go first!

your liking, lucky you! You're off the hook! However, if that dog spent his life up to this point in a kennel, or even in a good home but without any real training, be prepared to tackle the job ahead. A dog three years of age or older with no previous training cannot be blamed for not knowing what he was never taught. While the dog is trying to understand and learn your rules, at the same time he has to unlearn many of his previously self-taught habits and general view of the world.

Working with a professional trainer will speed up your progress with an adopted adult dog. You'll need patience, too. Some new rules may be close to impossible for the dog to accept. After all, he's been successful so far by doing everything his way! (Patience again.) He may agree with your instruction for a few days and then slip back into his old ways, so you must be just as consistent and understanding in your teaching as you would be with a puppy. (More patience needed yet again!) Your dog has to learn to pay attention to your voice, your family, the daily routine, new smells, new sounds and, in some cases, even a new climate.

One of the most important things to find out about a newly adopted adult dog is his reaction to children (yours and others), strangers and your friends, and how he acts upon meeting other dogs. If he was not socialized with dogs as a puppy,

this could be a major problem. This does not mean that he's a "bad" dog, a vicious dog or an aggressive dog; rather, it means that he has no idea how to read another dog's body language. There's no way for him to tell whether the other dog is a friend or foe. Survival instinct takes over, telling him to attack first and ask questions later. This definitely calls for professional help and, even then, may not be a behavior that can be corrected 100% reliably (or even at all). If you have a puppy, this is why it is so very important to introduce your young puppy properly to other puppies and "dog-friendly" adult dogs.

HOUSE-TRAINING YOUR NORWICH TERRIER

Dogs are "touch sensitive" when it comes to house-training. In other words, they respond to the surface on which they are given approval to eliminate. The choice is yours (the dog's version is in parentheses): The lawn (including the neighbors' lawns)? A bare patch of earth under a tree (where people like to sit and relax in the summertime)? Concrete steps or patio (all sidewalks, garages and basement floors)? The curbside (watch out for cars)? A small area of crushed stone in a corner of the yard (mine!)? The latter is the best choice if you can manage it, because it will remain

BASIC PRINCIPLES OF DOG TRAINING

1. Start training early. A young puppy is ready, willing and able.
2. Timing is your all-important tool. Praise at the exact time that the dog responds correctly. Pay close attention.
3. Patience is almost as important as timing!
4. Repeat! The same word has to mean the same thing every time.
5. In the beginning, praise all correct behavior verbally, along with treats and petting.

of play—all day long, from first thing in the morning until his bedtime! That's a total of ten or more trips per day to teach the puppy where it's okay to relieve himself. With that schedule in mind, you can see that house-training a young puppy is not a part-time job. It requires someone to be home all day.

If that seems overwhelming or impossible, do a little planning. For example, plan to pick up your puppy at the start of a vacation period. If you can't get home in the middle of the day, plan to hire a dog-sitter or ask a neighbor to come over to take the pup outside, feed him his lunch and then take him out again about ten or so minutes after he's eaten. Also make arrangements with that or another person to be your "emergency" contact if you have to stay late on the job. Remind yourself—repeatedly—that this hectic schedule improves as the puppy gets older.

strictly for the dog's use and is easy to keep clean.

You can start out with paper-training indoors and switch over to an outdoor surface as the puppy matures and gains control over his need to eliminate. For the nay-sayers, don't worry—this won't mean that the dog will soil on every piece of newspaper lying around the house. You are training him to go outside, remember? Starting out by paper-training often is the only choice for a city dog.

WHEN YOUR PUPPY'S "GOT TO GO"
Your puppy's need to relieve himself is seemingly non-stop, but signs of improvement will be seen each week. From 8 to 10 weeks old, the puppy will have to be taken outside every time he wakes up, about 10–15 minutes after every meal and after every period

Feeding and potty schedules are closely intertwined— what goes in must come out!

EXTRA! EXTRA!

The headlines read: "Puppy Piddles Here!" Breeders commonly use newspapers to line their whelping pens, so puppies learn to associate newspapers with relieving themselves. Do not use newspapers to line your pup's crate, as this will signal to your puppy that it is OK to urinate in his crate. If you choose to paper-train your puppy, you will layer newspapers on a section of the floor near the door he uses to go outside. You should encourage the puppy to use the papers to relieve himself, and bring him there whenever you see him getting ready to go. Little by little, you will reduce the size of the newspaper-covered area so that the puppy will learn to relieve himself "on the other side of the door."

HOME WITHIN A HOME

Your Norwich Terrier puppy needs to be confined to one secure, puppy-proof area when no one is able to watch his every move. Generally the kitchen is the place of choice because the floor is washable. Likewise, it's a busy family area that will accustom the pup to a variety of noises, everything from pots and pans to the telephone, blender and dishwasher. He will also be enchanted by the smell of your cooking (and will never be critical when you burn something). An exercise pen (also called an "ex-pen," a puppy version of a playpen) within the room of choice is an excellent means of confinement for a young pup. He can see out and has a certain amount of space in which to run about, but he is safe from dangerous things like electrical cords, heating units, trash baskets or open kitchen-supply cabinets. Place the pen where the puppy will not get a blast of heat or air conditioning.

In the pen, you can put a few toys, his bed (which can be his crate if the dimensions of pen and crate are compatible) and a few layers of newspaper in one small corner, just in case. A water bowl can be hung at a convenient height on the side of the ex-pen so it won't become a splashing pool for an innovative puppy. His food dish can go on the floor, near but not under the water bowl.

Crates are something that pet owners are at last getting used to for their dogs. Wild or domestic canines have always preferred to

CANINE DEVELOPMENT SCHEDULE

It is important to understand how and at what age a puppy develops into adulthood. If you are a puppy owner, consult the following Canine Development Schedule to determine the stage of development your puppy is currently experiencing. This knowledge will help you as you work with the puppy in the weeks and months ahead.

PERIOD	AGE	CHARACTERISTICS
FIRST TO THIRD	BIRTH TO SEVEN WEEKS	Puppy needs food, sleep and warmth and responds to simple and gentle touching. Needs mother for security and disciplining. Needs littermates for learning and interacting with other dogs. Pup learns to function within a pack and learns pack order of dominance. Begin socializing pup with adults and children for short periods. Pup begins to become aware of his environment.
FOURTH	EIGHT TO TWELVE WEEKS	Brain is fully developed. Pup needs socializing with outside world. Remove from mother and littermates. Needs to change from canine pack to human pack. Human dominance necessary. Fear period occurs between 8 and 12 weeks. Avoid fright and pain.
FIFTH	THIRTEEN TO SIXTEEN WEEKS	Training and formal obedience should begin. Less association with other dogs, more with people, places, situations. Period will pass easily if you remember this is pup's change-to-adolescence time. Be firm and fair. Flight instinct prominent. Permissiveness and over-disciplining can do permanent damage. Praise for good behavior.
JUVENILE	FOUR TO EIGHT MONTHS	Another fear period about 7 to 8 months of age. It passes quickly, but be cautious of fright and pain. Sexual maturity reached. Dominant traits established. Dog should understand sit, down, come and stay by now.

NOTE: THESE ARE APPROXIMATE TIME FRAMES. ALLOW FOR INDIVIDUAL DIFFERENCES IN PUPPIES.

sleep in den-like safe spots, and that is exactly what the crate provides. How often have you seen adult dogs that choose to sleep under a table or chair even though they have full run of the house? It's the den connection.

In your "happy" voice, use the word "Crate" every time you put the pup into his den. If he's new to a crate, toss in a small biscuit for him to chase the first few times. At night, after he's been outside, he should sleep in his crate. The crate may be kept in his designated area at night or, if you want to be sure to hear those wake-up yips in the morning, put the crate in a corner of your bedroom. However, don't make any response whatsoever to whining or crying. If he's completely ignored, he'll settle down and get to sleep.

Good bedding for a young puppy is an old folded bath towel or an old blanket, something that is easily washable and disposable if necessary ("accidents" will happen!). Never put newspaper in the puppy's crate. Also, those old ideas about adding a clock to replace his mother's heartbeat, or a hot-water bottle to replace her warmth, are just that—old ideas. The clock could drive the puppy nuts, and the hot-water bottle could end up as a very soggy waterbed! An extremely good breeder would have introduced your puppy to the crate by letting two pups sleep together for a couple of nights, followed by several nights alone. How thankful you will be if you found that breeder!

Safe toys in the pup's crate or area will keep him occupied, but monitor their condition closely. Discard any toys that show signs

DAILY SCHEDULE

How many relief trips does your puppy need per day? A puppy up to the age of 14 weeks will need to go outside about 8 to 12 times per day! You will have to take the pup out any time he starts sniffing around the floor or turning in small circles, as well as after naps, meals, games and lessons or whenever he's released from his crate. Once the puppy is 14 to 22 weeks of age, he will require only 6 to 8 relief trips. At the ages of 22 to 32 weeks, the puppy will require about 5 to 7 trips. Adult dogs typically require 4 relief trips per day, in the morning, afternoon, evening and late at night.

SOMEBODY TO BLAME

House-training a puppy can be frustrating for the puppy and the owner alike. The puppy does not instinctively understand the difference between defecating on the pavement outside and on the ceramic tile in the kitchen. He is confused and frightened by his human's exuberant reactions to his natural urges. The owner, arguably the more intelligent of the duo, is also frustrated that he cannot convince his puppy to obey his commands and instructions.

In frustration, the owner may struggle with the temptation to discipline the puppy, scold him or even strike him on the rear end. Not only are these harsh corrections unnecessary and inappropriate but they also will defeat your purpose in gaining your puppy's trust and respect. Don't blame your nine-week-old puppy. Blame yourself for not being 100% consistent in the puppy's lessons and routine. The lesson here is simple: try harder and your puppy will succeed.

have some free time with the family as long as there is someone responsible for watching him. That doesn't mean just someone in the same room who is watching TV or busy on the computer, but one person who is doing nothing other than keeping an eye on the pup, playing with him on the floor and helping him understand his position in the pack.

This first taste of freedom will let you begin to set the house rules. If you don't want the dog on the furniture, now is the time to prevent his first attempts to jump up onto the couch. The word to use in this case is "Off," not "Down." "Down" is the word you will use to teach the down position, which is something entirely different.

Most corrections at this stage come in the form of simply distracting the puppy. Instead of

Your Norwich will learn to relieve himself on the surface that you choose. Grass is the most common choice, though city dwellers may be forced to choose newspaper or pavement.

of being chewed to bits. Squeaky parts, bits of stuffing or plastic or any other small pieces can cause intestinal blockage or possibly choking if swallowed.

PROGRESSING WITH POTTY-TRAINING

After you've taken your puppy out and he has relieved himself in the area you've selected, he can

telling him "No" for "Don't chew the carpet," distract the chomping puppy with a toy and he'll forget about the carpet.

As you are playing with the pup, do not forget to watch him closely and pay attention to his body language. Whenever you see him begin to circle or sniff, take the puppy outside to relieve himself. If you are paper-training, put him back into his confined area on the newspapers. In either case, praise him as he eliminates while he actually is *in the act* of relieving himself. Three seconds after he has finished is too late!

You'll be praising him for running toward you, or picking up a toy or whatever he may be doing at that moment, and that's not what you want to be praising him for. Timing is a vital tool in all dog training. Use it.

Remove soiled newspapers immediately and replace them with clean ones. You may want to take a small piece of soiled paper and place it in the middle of the new clean papers, as the scent will attract him to that spot when it's time to go again. That scent attraction is why it's so important to clean up any messes made in

Much of a newborn puppy's daily activity takes place within the whelping box. As he grows, separate areas for eating, sleeping and relieving himself are introduced.

the house by using a product specially made to eliminate the odor of dog urine and droppings. Regular household cleansers won't do the trick. Pet shops sell the best pet deodorizers. Invest in the largest container you can find.

Scent attraction eventually will lead your pup to his chosen spot outdoors; this is the basis of outdoor training. When you take your puppy outside to relieve himself, use a one-word command such as "Outside" or "Go-potty" (that's one word to the puppy!) as

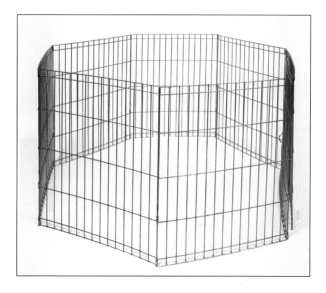

A wire "ex-pen" is a helpful tool for providing your pup with an area of safe confinement.

LEASH TRAINING

House-training and leash training go hand in hand, literally. When taking your puppy outside to do his business, lead him there on his leash. Unless an emergency potty run is called for, do not whisk the puppy up into your arms and take him outside. If you have a fenced yard, you have the advantage of letting the puppy loose to go out, but it's better to put the dog on the leash and take him to his designated place in the yard until he is reliably house-trained. Taking the puppy for a walk is the best way to house-train a dog. The dog will associate the walk with his time to relieve himself, and the exercise of walking stimulates the dog's bowels and bladder. Dogs that are not trained to relieve themselves on a walk may hold it until they get back home, which of course defeats half the purpose of the walk.

you pick him up and attach his leash. Then put him down in his area. If for any reason you can't carry him, snap the leash on quickly and lead him to his spot. Now comes the hard part—hard for you, that is. Just stand there until he urinates and defecates. Move him a few feet in one direction or another if he's just sitting there looking at you, but remember that this is neither playtime nor time for a walk. This is strictly a business trip! Then, as he circles and squats (remember your timing!), give him a quiet "Good dog" as praise. If you start to jump for joy, ecstatic over his performance, he'll do one of two things: either he will stop mid-stream, as it were, or he'll do it again for you—in the house—and expect you to be just as delighted!

Male dogs tend to be more fixated on their toileting needs, frequently stopping at every vertical object to leave their special mark.

ment is needed. You and your puppy are just learning each other's language, and sometimes it's easy to miss a puppy's message. Chalk it up to experience and watch more closely from now on.

KEEPING THE PACK ORDERLY
Discipline is a form of training that brings order to life. For example, military discipline is what allows the soldiers in an army to work as one. Discipline is a form of teaching and, in dogs, is the basis of how the successful pack operates. Each member knows his place in the pack and all respect the leader, or Alpha dog. It is essential for your puppy that you establish this type of relationship, with you as the

Give him five minutes or so and, if he doesn't go in that time, take him back indoors to his confined area and try again in another ten minutes, or immediately if you see him sniffing and circling. By careful observation, you'll soon work out a successful schedule.

Accidents, by the way, are just that—accidents. Clean them up quickly and thoroughly, without comment, after the puppy has been taken outside to finish his business and then put back into his area or crate. If you witness an accident in progress, say "No!" in a stern voice and get the pup outdoors immediately. No punish-

---

SMILE WHEN YOU ORDER ME AROUND!
While trainers recommend practicing with your dog every day, it's perfectly acceptable to take a "mental health day" off. It's better not to train the dog on days when you're in a sour mood. Your bad attitude or lack of interest will be sensed by your dog, and he will respond accordingly. Studies show that dogs are well tuned in to their humans' emotions. Be conscious of how you use your voice when talking to your dog. Raising your voice or shouting will only erode your dog's trust in you as his trainer and master.

Alpha, or leader. It is a form of social coexistence that all canines recognize and accept. Discipline, therefore, is never to be confused with punishment. When you teach your puppy how you want him to behave, and he behaves properly and you praise him for it, you are disciplining him with a form of positive reinforcement.

For a dog, rewards come in the form of praise, a smile, a cheerful tone of voice, a few friendly pats or a rub of the ears. Rewards are also small food treats. Obviously, that does not mean bits of regular dog food. Instead, treats are very small bits of special things like cheese or pieces of soft dog treats. The idea is to reward the dog with something very small that he can taste and swallow, providing instant positive reinforcement. If he has to take time to chew the treat, by the time he is finished he will have forgotten what he did to earn it!

Your puppy should never be physically punished. The displeasure shown on your face and in your voice is sufficient to signal to the pup that he has done something wrong. He wants to please everyone higher up on the social ladder, especially his leader, so a scowl and harsh voice will take care of the error. Growling out the word "Shame!" when the pup is caught in the act of doing something wrong is

better than the repetitive "No." Some dogs hear "No" so often that they begin to think it's their name! By the way, do not use the dog's name when you're correcting him. His name is reserved to get his attention for something pleasant about to take place.

There are punishments that have nothing to do with you. For

BE UPSTANDING!
You are the dog's leader. During training, stand up straight so your dog looks up at you, and therefore up *to* you. Say the command words distinctly, in a clear, declarative tone of voice. (No barking!) Give rewards only as the correct response takes place (remember your timing!). Praise, smiles and treats are "rewards" used to positively reinforce correct responses. Don't repeat a mistake. Just change to another exercise—you will soon find success!

example, your dog may think that chasing cats is one reason for his existence. You can try to stop it as much as you like but without success, because it's such fun for the dog. But one good hissing, spitting swipe of a cat's claws across the dog's nose will put an end to the game forever. Intervene only when your dog's eyeball is seriously at risk. Cat scratches can cause permanent damage to an innocent but annoying puppy.

PUPPY KINDERGARTEN

COLLAR AND LEASH

Before you begin your Norwich Terrier puppy's education, he must be used to his collar and leash. Choose a collar for your puppy that is secure, but not heavy or bulky. He won't enjoy training if he's uncomfortable. A flat buckle collar is fine for everyday wear and for initial puppy training. For older dogs, there are several types of training collars such as the martingale, which is a double loop that tightens slightly around the neck, or the head collar, which is

---

TIME TO PLAY!

Playtime can happen both indoors and out. A young puppy is growing so rapidly that he needs sleep more than he needs a lot of physical exercise. Puppies get sufficient exercise on their own just through normal puppy activity. Monitor play with young children so you can remove the puppy when he's had enough, or calm the kids if they get too rowdy. Almost all puppies love to chase after a toy you've thrown, and you can turn your games into educational activities. Every time your puppy brings the toy back to you, say "Give it" (or "Drop it") followed by "Good dog" and throwing it again. If he's reluctant to give it to you, offer a small treat so that he drops the toy as he takes the treat. He will soon get the idea.

similar to a horse's halter. Do not use a chain choke collar with your Norwich Terrier. Ask your breeder about suitable training collars for the breed.

A lightweight 6-foot woven cotton or nylon training leash is preferred by most trainers because it is easy to fold up in your hand and comfortable to hold because there is a certain amount of give to it. There are lessons where the dog will start off 6 feet away from you at the end of the leash. The leash used to take the puppy outside to relieve himself is shorter because you don't want him to roam away from his area. The shorter leash will also be the one to use when you walk the puppy.

If you've been wise enough to enroll in a Puppy Kindergarten training class, suggestions will be made as to the best collar and leash for your young puppy. I say "wise" because your puppy will be in a class with puppies in his age range (up to five months old) of all breeds and sizes. It's the perfect way for him to learn the right way (and the wrong way) to interact with other dogs as well as their people. You cannot teach your puppy how to interpret another dog's sign language. For a first-time puppy owner, these socialization classes are invaluable. For experienced dog owners, they are a real boon to further training.

ATTENTION

You've been using the dog's name since the minute you collected him from the breeder, so you should be able to get his attention by saying his name—with a big smile and in an excited tone of voice. His response will be the puppy equivalent of "Here I am! What are we going to do?" Your immediate response (if you haven't guessed by now) is "Good dog." Rewarding him at the moment he pays attention to you teaches him the proper way to respond when he hears his name.

EXERCISES FOR A BASIC CANINE EDUCATION

THE SIT EXERCISE

There are several ways to teach the puppy to sit. The first one is to catch him whenever he is about

Praise and a tasty morsel are the keys to the Norwich's kingdom—and the keys to your training success!

to sit and, as his backside nears the floor, say "Sit, good dog!" That's positive reinforcement and, if your timing is sharp, he will learn that what he's doing at that second is connected to your saying "Sit" and that you think he's clever for doing it!

Another method is to start with the puppy on his leash in front of you. Show him a treat in the palm of your right hand. Bring your hand up under his nose and, almost in slow motion, move your hand up and back so his nose goes up in the air and his head tilts back as he follows the treat in your hand. At that point, he will have to either sit or fall over, so as his back legs buckle under, say "Sit, good dog," and then give him the treat and lots of praise. You may have to begin with your hand lightly running up his chest, actually lifting his chin up until he sits. Some (usually older) dogs require gentle pressure on their hindquarters with the left hand, in which case the dog should be on your left side. Puppies generally do not appreciate this physical dominance.

After a few times, you should be able to show the dog a treat in the open palm of your hand, raise your hand waist-high as you say "Sit" and have him sit. You will thereby have taught him two things at the same time. Both the verbal command and the motion of the hand are signals for the sit.

Your puppy is watching you almost more than he is listening to you, so what you do is just as important as what you say.

Don't save any of these drills only for training sessions. Use them as much as possible at odd times during a normal day. The dog should always sit before being given his food dish. He should sit to let you go through a doorway first, when the doorbell rings or when you stop to speak to someone on the street.

THE DOWN EXERCISE
Before beginning to teach the down command, you must consider how the dog feels about this exercise. To him, "down" is a submissive position. Being flat on the floor with you standing over him is not his idea of fun. It's up to you to let him know that, while it may not be fun, the reward of

READY, SIT, GO!
On your marks, get set: train! Most professional trainers agree that the sit command is the place to start your dog's formal education. Sitting is a natural posture for most dogs, and they respond to the sit exercise willingly and readily. For every lesson, begin with the sit command so that you start out with a successful exercise; likewise, you should practice the sit command at the end of every lesson as well, because you always want to end on a high note.

SAY IT SIMPLY

When you command your dog to sit, use the word "Sit." Do not say "Sit down," as your dog will not know whether you mean "Sit" or "Down," or maybe you mean both. Be clear in your instructions to your dog; use one-word commands and always be consistent.

your approval is worth his effort.

Start with the puppy on your left side in a sit position. Hold the leash right above his collar in your left hand. Have an extra-special treat, such as a small piece of cooked chicken or hot dog, in your right hand. Place it at the end of the pup's nose and steadily move your hand down and forward along the ground. Hold the leash to prevent a sudden lunge for the food. As the puppy goes into the down position, say "Down" very gently.

The difficulty with this exercise is twofold: it's both the submissive aspect and the fact that most people say the word "Down" as if they were a drill sergeant in charge of recruits! So issue the command sweetly, give him the treat and have the pup maintain the down position for several seconds. If he tries to get up immediately, place your hands on his shoulders and press down gently, giving him a very quiet "Good dog." As you progress with

this lesson, increase the "down time" until he will hold it until you say "Okay" (his cue for release). Practice this one in the house at various times throughout the day.

By increasing the length of time during which the dog must maintain the down position, you'll find many uses for it. For example, he can lie at your feet in the vet's office or anywhere that both of you have to wait, when you are on the phone, while the family is eating and so forth. If you progress to training for competitive obedience, he'll already be all set for the exercise called the "long down."

THE STAY EXERCISE

You can teach your Norwich Terrier to stay in the sit, down and stand positions. To teach the sit/stay, have the dog sit on your left side. Hold the leash at waist level in your left hand and let the dog know that you have a treat in your closed right hand. Step forward on your right foot as you say "Stay." Immediately turn and stand directly in front of the dog, keeping your right hand up high so he'll keep his eye on the treat hand and maintain the sit position for a count of five. Return to your original position and offer the reward.

Increase the length of the sit/stay each time until the dog can hold it for at least 30 seconds without moving. After about a week of success, move out on your right foot and take two steps before turning to face the dog. Give the "Stay" hand signal (left palm back toward the dog's head) as you leave. He gets the treat when you return and he holds the sit/stay. Increase the distance that you walk away from him before turning until you reach the length of your training leash. But don't rush it! Go back to the beginning if he moves before he should. No matter what the lesson, never be upset by having to back up for a few days. The repetition and practice are what will make your dog reliable in these commands. It won't do any good to move on to something more difficult if the command is not mastered at the easier levels. Above all, even if you do get frustrated, never let your puppy know! Always keep a positive, upbeat attitude during

The "stay" hand signal reinforces the verbal command that tells the dog not to move from his position, whether sitting, lying down or standing.

> ## OKAY!
> This is the signal that tells your dog that he can quit whatever he was doing. Use "Okay" to end a session on a correct response to a command. (Never end on an incorrect response.) Lots of praise follows. People use "Okay" a lot and it has other uses for dogs, too. Your dog is barking. You say, "Okay! Come!" "Okay" signals him to stop the barking activity and "Come" allows him to come to you for a "Good dog."

training, which will transmit to your dog for positive results.

The down/stay is taught in the same way once the dog is completely reliable and steady with the down command. Again, don't rush it. With the dog in the down position on your left side, step out on your right foot as you say "Stay." Return by walking around in back of the dog and into your original position. While you are training, it's okay to murmur something like "Hold on" to encourage him to stay put. When the dog will stay without moving when you are at a distance of 3 or 4 feet, begin to increase the length of time before you return. Be sure he holds the down on your return until you say "Okay." At that point, he gets his treat—just so he'll remember for next time that it's not over until it's over.

THE COME EXERCISE

No command is more important to the safety of your Norwich Terrier than "Come." It is what you should say every single time you see the puppy running toward you: "Binky, come! Good dog." During playtime, run a few feet away from the puppy and turn and tell him to "Come" as he is already running to you. You can go so far as to teach your puppy two things at once if you squat down and hold out your arms. As the pup gets close to you and

you're saying "Good dog," bring your right arm in about waist high. Now he's also learning the hand signal, an excellent device should you be on the phone when you need to get him to come to you! You'll also both be one step ahead when you enter obedience classes.

When the puppy responds to your well-timed "Come," try it with the puppy on the training leash. This time, catch him off-guard, while he's sniffing a leaf or watching a bird: "Binky, come!" You may have to pause for a split second after his name to be sure you have his attention. If the puppy shows any sign of confusion, give the leash a mild jerk and take a couple of steps backward. Do not repeat the command. In this case, you should say "Good come" as he reaches you.

That's the number-one rule of

Coming when called is not one of the Norwich's specialties! Once the dog gets a scent in his nose or an idea in his head, it's difficult to recall this active terrier. Invest real effort in teaching the come command.

TIPS FOR TRAINING AND SAFETY

1. Whether on- or off-leash, practice only in a fenced area.
2. Remove the training collar when the training session is over.
3. Don't try to break up a dog fight.
4. "Come," "Leave it" and "Wait" are safety commands.
5. The dog belongs in a crate or behind a barrier when riding in the car.
6. Don't ignore the dog's first sign of aggression. Aggression only gets worse, so take it seriously.
7. Keep the faces of children and dogs separated.
8. Pay attention to what the dog is chewing.
9. Keep the vet's number near your phone.
10. "Okay" is a useful release command.

DON'T STRESS ME OUT
Your dog doesn't have to deal with paying the bills, the daily commute, PTA meetings and the like, but, believe it or not, there's a lot of stress in a dog's world. Stress can be caused by the owner's impatient demeanor and his angry or harsh corrections. If your dog cringes when you reach for his training collar, he's stressed. An older dog is sometimes stressed out when he goes to a new home. No matter what the cause, put off all training until he's over it. If he's going through a fear period—shying away from people, trembling when spoken to, avoiding eye contact or hiding under furniture—wait to resume training. Naturally you'd also postpone your lessons if the dog were sick, and the same goes for you. Show some compassion.

training. Each command word is given just once. Anything more is nagging. You'll also notice that all commands are one word only. Even when they are actually two words, you say them as one.

Never call the dog to come to you—with or without his name— if you are angry or intend to correct him for some misbehavior. When correcting the pup, you go to him. Your dog must always connect "Come" with something pleasant and with your approval; then you can rely on his response.

Puppies, like children, have notoriously short attention spans, so don't overdo it with any of the training. Keep each lesson short. Break it up with a quick run around the yard or a ball toss, repeat the lesson and quit as soon as the pup gets it right. That way, you will always end with a "Good dog."

Life isn't perfect and neither are puppies. A time will come, often around ten months of age, when he'll become "selectively deaf" or choose to "forget" his name. He may respond by wagging his tail (and even seeming to smile at you) with a look that says "Make me!" Laugh, throw his favorite toy and skip the lesson you had planned. Pups will be pups!

THE HEEL EXERCISE
The second most important command to teach, after the come, is the heel. When you are walking your growing puppy, you need to be in control. Besides, it looks terrible to get all tangled up in the leash, and it's not much fun either. Your eight- to ten-week-old puppy will probably follow you everywhere, but that's his natural instinct, not your control over the situation. However, any time he does follow you, you can say "Heel" and be ahead of the game, as he will learn to associate this command with the action of following you before you even begin teaching him to heel.

LET'S GO!

Many people use "Let's go" instead of "Heel" when teaching their dogs to behave on lead. It sounds more like fun! When beginning to teach the heel, whatever command you use, always step off on your left foot. That's the one next to the dog, who is on your left side, in case you've forgotten. Keep a loose leash. When the dog pulls ahead, stop, bring him back and begin again. Use treats to guide him around turns.

There is a very precise, almost military, procedure for teaching your dog to heel. As with all other obedience training, begin with the dog on your left side. He will be in a very nice sit and you will have the training leash across your chest. Hold the loop and folded leash in your right hand. Pick up the slack leash above the dog in your left hand and hold it loosely at your side. Step out on your left foot as you say "Heel." If the puppy does not move, give a gentle tug or pat your left leg to get him started. If he surges ahead of you, stop and pull him back gently until he is at your side. Tell him to sit and begin again.

Walk a few steps and stop while the puppy is correctly beside you. Tell him to sit and give mild verbal praise. (More enthusiastic praise will encourage him to think the lesson is over.)

Repeat the lesson, increasing the number of steps you take only as long as the dog is heeling nicely beside you. When you end the lesson, have him hold the sit, then give him the "Okay" to let him know that this is the end of the lesson. Praise him so that he knows he did a good job.

The cure for excessive pulling (a common problem) is to stop when the dog is no more than 2 or 3 feet ahead of you. Guide him back into position and begin again. With a really determined puller, try switching to a head collar. This will automatically turn the pup's head toward you so

Two Norwich will mean training times two. Daily walks would be quite a chore if this pair had not been taught to behave on lead.

NO MORE TREATS!
When your dog is responding promptly and correctly to commands, it's time to eliminate treats. Begin by alternating a treat reward with a verbal-praise-only reward. Gradually eliminate all treats while increasing the frequency of praise. Overlook pleading eyes and expectant expressions, but if he's still watching your treat hand, you're on your way to using hand signals.

you can bring him back easily to the heel position. Give quiet, reassuring praise every time the leash goes slack and he's staying with you.

Staying and heeling can take a lot out of a dog, so provide playtime and free-running exercise to shake off the stress when the lessons are over. You don't want him to associate training with all work and no fun.

OBEDIENCE CLASSES
The advantages of an obedience class are that your dog will have to learn amid the distractions of other people and dogs and that your mistakes will be quickly corrected by the trainer. Teaching your dog along with a qualified instructor and other handlers who may have more dog experience than you is another plus of the class environment. The instructor and other handlers can help you to find the most efficient way of teaching your dog a command or exercise. It's often easier to learn from other people's mistakes than your own. You will also learn all of the requirements for competitive obedience trials, in which you can earn titles and go on to advanced jumping and retrieving exercises, which are fun for many dogs. Obedience classes build the foundation needed for many other canine activities (in which we humans are allowed to participate, too!).

WHO'S TRAINING WHOM?

Dog training is a black-and-white exercise. The correct response to a command must be absolute, and the trainer must insist on completely accurate responses from the dog. A trainer cannot command his dog to sit and then settle for the dog's melting into the down position. Often owners are so pleased that their dogs "did something" in response to a command that they just shrug and say, "OK, Down" even though they wanted the dog to sit. You want your dog to respond to the command without hesitation: he must respond at that moment and correctly every time.

TRAINING FOR OTHER ACTIVITIES

If you are interested in partici-pating in organized competition with your Norwich, there are activities other than obedience in which you and your dog can become involved. For a terrier as enthusiastic as the Norwich, earthdog trials fit the bill quite nicely. These trials are designed to test the terrier's ability to go to ground, in pursuit of quarry that burrow into dens. The American Kennel Club and the American Working Terrier Association sponsor earthdog tests. The tests have several levels and become increasingly difficult as the dog learns to scent the quarry, unearth the den and fearlessly locate his quarry. The quarry is caged and therefore is not physically harmed, as the dog cannot actually get to it.

With a breed this talented and energetic, there is no limit to the activities that the Norwich Terrier owner can pursue. Tracking events, scent hurdle races, flyball and agility are just some of the possibilities. Agility, the most popular of these, engages the dogs to run through obstacle courses that include various jumps, tunnels and other exercises to test the dog's speed and coordination. Obstacles are adjusted according

Show dogs must demonstrate their ability to heel in the ring as the judge evaluates their gait.

A true earthdog, your Norwich will quickly get into every corner of the yard to which he has access.

to the height of the dogs, so that the small dogs can compete on a level playing field (though it's best not to let your Norwich know that he's small—he certainly doesn't know it!). The owners run beside their dogs to give commands and to guide them through the course. Although competitive, the focus is on fun—it's fun to do, fun to watch and great exercise.

For those who like to volunteer, there is the wonderful feeling of owning a therapy dog and visiting hospices, nursing homes and veterans' homes to bring smiles, comfort and companionship to those who live there. Around the house, your Norwich Terrier can be taught to do some simple chores. You might teach him to carry a basket of household items or to fetch the morning newspaper. The kids can teach the dog all kinds of tricks, from playing hide-and-seek to balancing a biscuit on his nose. A family dog is what rounds out the family. Everything he does, including sitting in your lap and gazing lovingly at you, represents the bonus of owning a dog.

NORWICH TERRIER

By Lowell Ackerman DVM, DACVD

HEALTHCARE FOR A LIFETIME

When you own a dog, you become his healthcare advocate over his entire lifespan, as well as being the one to shoulder the financial burden of such care. Accordingly, it is worthwhile to focus on prevention rather than treatment, as you and your pet will both be happier.

Of course, the best place to have begun your program of preventive healthcare is with the initial purchase or adoption of your dog. There is no way of guaranteeing that your new furry friend is free of medical problems, but there are some things you can do to improve your odds. You certainly should have done adequate research into the Norwich Terrier and have selected your puppy carefully rather than buying on impulse. Health issues aside, a large number of pet abandonment and relinquishment cases arise from a mismatch between pet needs and owner expectations. This is entirely preventable with appropriate planning and finding a good breeder.

Regarding healthcare issues specifically, it is very difficult to make blanket statements about where to acquire a problem-free pet, but, again, a reputable breeder is your best bet. In an ideal situation, you have the opportunity to see both parents, get references from other owners of the breeder's pups and see genetic-testing documentation for several generations of the litter's ancestors. At the very least, you must thoroughly investigate the Norwich Terrier and the problems inherent in that breed, as well as the genetic testing available to screen for those problems. Genetic testing offers some important benefits, but testing is available for only a few disorders in a relatively small number of breeds and is not available for some of the most common genetic diseases, such as hip dysplasia, cataracts, epilepsy, cardiomy-opathy, etc. This area of research is indeed exciting and increasingly important, and advances will continue to be made each year. In fact, recent research has shown that there is an equivalent dog gene for 75% of known human genes, so research done in either species is likely to benefit the other.

We've also discussed that evaluating the behavioral nature

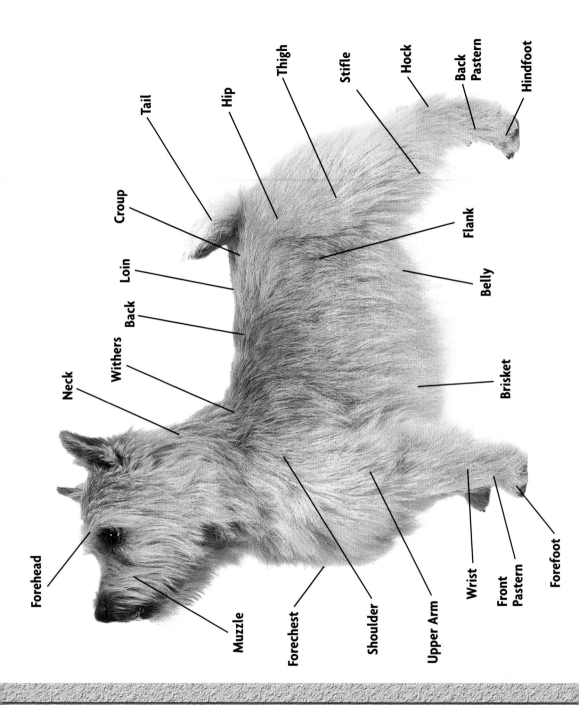

Forehead

Neck

Withers

Back

Loin

Croup

Tail

Hip

Thigh

Stifle

Hock

Back Pastern

Hindfoot

Flank

Belly

Brisket

Muzzle

Forechest

Shoulder

Upper Arm

Wrist

Front Pastern

Forefoot

PHYSICAL STRUCTURE OF THE NORWICH TERRIER

of your Norwich Terrier and that of his immediate family members is an important part of the selection process that cannot be underestimated or overemphasized. It is sometimes difficult to evaluate temperament in puppies because certain behavioral tendencies, such as some forms of aggression, may not be immediately evident. More dogs are euthanized each year for behavioral reasons than for all medical conditions combined, so it is critical to take temperament issues seriously. Start with a well-balanced, friendly companion and put the time and effort into proper socialization, and you will both be rewarded with a lifelong valued relationship.

Assuming that you have started off with a pup from healthy, sound stock, you then become responsible for helping your veterinarian keep your pet healthy. Some crucial things happen before you even bring your puppy home. Parasite control typically begins at two weeks of age, and vaccinations typically begin at six to eight weeks of age. A pre-pubertal evaluation is typically scheduled for about six months of age. At this time, a dental evaluation is done (since the adult teeth are now in), heartworm prevention is started and neutering or spaying is most commonly done.

It is critical to commence

DOGGIE DENTAL DON'TS

A veterinary dental exam is necessary if you notice one or any combination of the following in your dog:
- Broken, loose or missing teeth
- Loss of appetite (which could be due to mouth pain or illness caused by infection)
- Gum abnormalities, including redness, swelling and bleeding
- Drooling, with or without blood
- Yellowing of the teeth or gumline, indicating tartar
- Bad breath

regular dental care at home if you have not already done so. It may not sound very important, but most dogs have active periodontal disease by four years of age if they don't have their teeth cleaned regularly at home, not just at their veterinary exams. Dental problems lead to more than just bad "doggie breath." Gum disease can have very serious medical consequences. If you start brushing your dog's teeth and using antiseptic rinses from a young age, your dog will be accustomed to it and will not resist. The results will be healthy dentition, which your pet will need to enjoy a long, healthy life. If you neglect your Norwich's teeth and he needs a veterinary tooth-scraping, he will need anesthesia, something you want to to avoid with the breed. So be

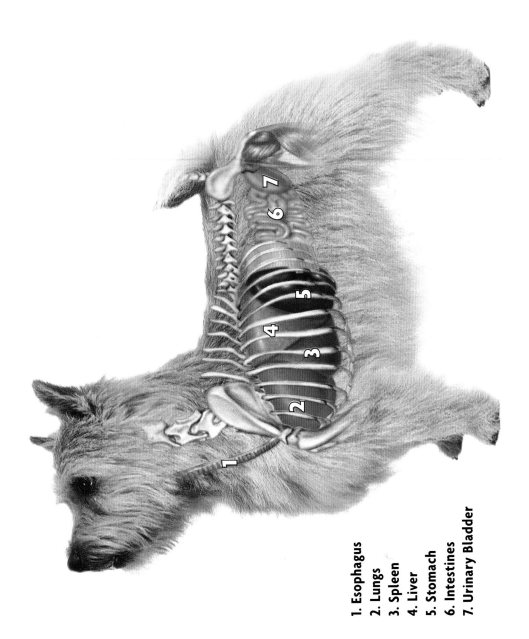

1. Esophagus
2. Lungs
3. Spleen
4. Liver
5. Stomach
6. Intestines
7. Urinary Bladder

INTERNAL ORGANS OF THE NORWICH TERRIER

proactive with his dental care from the start!

Most dogs are considered adults at a year of age, although some larger breeds still have some filling out to do up to about two or so years old. Even individual dogs within each breed have different healthcare requirements, so work with your veterinarian to determine what will be needed and what your role should be. This doctor-client relationship is

TAKING YOUR DOG'S TEMPERATURE

It is important to know how to take your dog's temperature at times when you think he may be ill. It's not the most enjoyable task, but it can be done without too much difficulty. It's easier with a helper, preferably someone with whom the dog is friendly, so that one of you can hold the dog while the other inserts the thermometer.

Before inserting the thermometer, coat the end with petroleum jelly. Insert the thermometer slowly and gently into the dog's rectum about one inch. Wait for the reading, about two minutes. Be sure to remove the thermometer carefully and clean it thoroughly after each use.

A dog's normal body temperature is between 100.5 and 102.5 degrees F. Immediate veterinary attention is required if the dog's temperature is below 99 or above 104 degrees F.

important, because as vaccination guidelines change, there may not be an annual "vaccine visit" scheduled. You must make sure that you see your veterinarian at least annually, even if no vaccines are due, because this is the best opportunity to coordinate health-care activities and to make sure that no medical issues creep by unaddressed.

When your Norwich Terrier reaches three-quarters of his anticipated lifespan, he is considered a "senior" and likely requires some special care. In general, if you've been taking great care of your canine companion throughout his formative and adult years, the transition to senior status should be a smooth one. Age is not a disease, and as long as everything is functioning as it should, there is no reason why most of late adulthood should not be rewarding for both you and your pet. This is especially true if you have tended to the details, such as regular veterinary visits, proper dental care, excellent nutrition and management of bone and joint issues.

As your Norwich approaches his senior years, your veterinarian may want to schedule visits twice yearly, instead of once, to run some laboratory screenings, electrocardiograms and the like, and to change the diet to something more digestible.

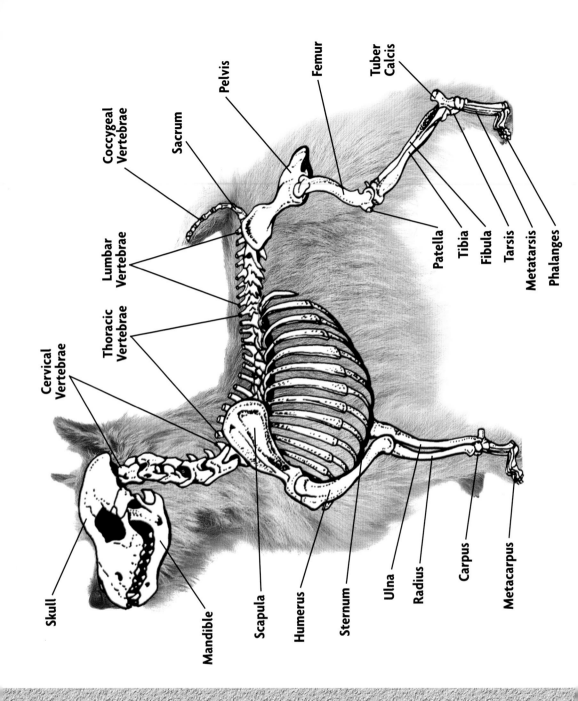

Cervical Vertebrae

Thoracic Vertebrae

Lumbar Vertebrae

Coccygeal Vertebrae

Sacrum

Pelvis

Femur

Tuber Calcis

Patella

Tibia

Fibula

Tarsis

Metatarsis

Phalanges

Skull

Mandible

Scapula

Humerus

Sternum

Ulna

Radius

Carpus

Metacarpus

SKELETAL STRUCTURE OF THE NORWICH TERRIER

Catching problems early is the best way to manage them effectively. Treating the early stages of heart disease is so much easier than trying to intervene when there is more significant damage to the heart muscle. Similarly, managing the beginning of kidney problems is fairly routine if there is no significant kidney damage. Other problems, like cognitive dysfunction (similar to senility and Alzheimer's disease), cancer, diabetes and arthritis, are more common in older dogs, but all can be treated to help the dog live as many happy, comfortable years as possible. Just as in people, medical management is more effective (and less expensive) when you catch things early.

SELECTING A VETERINARIAN
There is probably no more important decision that you will make regarding your pet's health-care than the selection of his doctor. Your pet's veterinarian will be a pediatrician, family-practice physician and gerontologist, depending on the dog's life stage, and will be the individual who makes recommendations regarding issues such as when specialists need to be consulted, when diagnostic testing and/or therapeutic intervention is needed and when you will need to seek outside emergency and critical-care services. Your vet will act as

YOUR DOG NEEDS TO VISIT THE VET IF:
- He has ingested a toxin such as antifreeze or a toxic plant; in these cases, administer first aid and call the vet right away
- His teeth are discolored, loose or missing or he has sores or other signs of infection or abnormality in the mouth
- He has been vomiting, has had diarrhea or has been constipated for over 24 hours; call immediately if you notice blood
- He has refused food for over 24 hours
- His eating habits, water intake or toilet habits have noticeably changed; if you have noticed weight gain or weight loss
- He shows symptoms of bloat, which requires *immediate* attention
- He is salivating excessively
- He has a lump in his throat
- He has lumps or bumps anywhere on the body
- He is very lethargic
- He appears to be in pain or otherwise has trouble chewing or swallowing
- His skin loses elasticity.

Of course, there will be other instances in which a visit to the vet is necessary; these are just some of the signs that could be indicative of serious problems that need to be caught as early as possible.

your advocate and liaison throughout these processes.

Everyone has his own idea about what to look for in a vet, an individual who will play a big role in his dog's (and, of course, his own) life for many years to come. For some, it is the compassionate caregiver with whom they hope to develop a professional relationship to span the lives of their dogs and even their future pets. For others, they are seeking a clinician with keen diagnostic and therapeutic insight who can deliver state-of-the-art healthcare. Still others need a veterinary

BEWARE THE SPIDER

Should you worry about having a spider spinning her mucilaginous web over your dog? Like other venomous critters, spiders can bite dogs and cause severe reactions. The most deleterious eight-leggers are the black and red widows, brown recluse and common brown spiders, whose bites can cause local pain, cramping, spasms and restlessness. These signals tell owners there is a problem, as the bites themselves can be difficult to locate under your dog's coat. Another vicious arachnid is the bark scorpion, whose bite can cause excessive drooling, tearing, urination and defecation. Often spider and scorpion bites are misdiagnosed because vets don't recognize the signs and owners didn't witness the escape of the avenging arachnid.

facility that is open evenings and weekends, is in close proximity or provides mobile veterinary services to accommodate their schedules; these people may not much mind that their dogs might see different veterinarians on each visit. Just as we have different reasons for selecting our own healthcare professionals (e.g., covered by insurance plan, expert in field, convenient location, etc.), we should not expect that there is a one-size-fits-all recommendation for selecting a veterinarian and veterinary practice. The best advice is to be honest in your assessment of what you expect from a veterinary practice and to conscientiously research the options in your area. You will quickly appreciate that not all veterinary practices are the same, and you will be happiest with one that truly meets your needs. You want a vet who is familiar with the Norwich or at least one with whom you feel comfortable discussing breed-specific issues like anesthesia, safe vaccinations, etc.

There is another point to be considered in the selection of veterinary services. Not that long ago, a single veterinarian would attempt to manage all medical and surgical issues as they arose. That was often problematic, because veterinarians are trained in many species and many diseases, and it was just impossible for general veterinary practitioners to be experts in every species, every breed, every field and every ailment. However, just as in the human healthcare fields, specialization has allowed general practitioners to concentrate on primary healthcare delivery, especially wellness and the prevention of infectious diseases, and to utilize a network of specialists to assist in the management of conditions that require specific expertise and experience. Thus there are now many types of veterinary specialists, including dermatologists, cardiologists, ophthalmologists, surgeons, internists, oncologists, neurologists, behaviorists, criticalists and others to help primary-care veterinarians deal with complicated medical challenges. In most cases, specialists see cases referred by primary-care veterinarians, make diagnoses and set up management plans. From there, the animals' ongoing care is returned to their primary-care veterinarians. This important team approach to your pet's medical-care needs has provided opportunities for advanced care and an unparalleled level of quality to be delivered.

With all of the opportunities for your Norwich Terrier to receive high-quality veterinary medical care, there is another topic that needs to be addressed at the same time—cost. It's been said that you can have excellent

FOOD INTOLERANCE

Food intolerance is the inability of the dog to completely digest certain foods. This occurs because the dog does not have the chemicals necessary to digest some foodstuffs. These chemicals are called enzymes. All puppies have the enzymes necessary to digest canine milk, but some dogs do not have the enzymes to digest a very different form of milk that is commonly found in human households—milk from cows. This is true in the Norwich Terrier, as some cannot tolerate dairy products. In such dogs, drinking cows' milk results in loose bowels, stomach pains and the passage of gas.

healthcare or inexpensive healthcare, but never both; this is as true in veterinary medicine as it is in human medicine. While veterinary costs are a fraction of what the same services cost in the human healthcare arena, it is still difficult to deal with unanticipated medical costs, especially since they can easily creep into hundreds or even thousands of dollars if specialists or emergency services become involved. However, there are ways of managing these risks. The easiest is to buy pet health insurance and realize that its foremost purpose is not to cover routine healthcare visits but rather to serve as an umbrella for those rainy days

COMMON INFECTIOUS DISEASES

Let's discuss some of the diseases that create the need for vaccination in the first place. Following are the major canine infectious diseases and a simple explanation of each.

Rabies: A devastating viral disease that can be fatal in dogs and people. In fact, vaccination of dogs and cats is an important public-health measure to create a resistant animal buffer population to protect people from contracting the disease. Vaccination schedules are determined on a government level and are not optional for pet owners; rabies vaccination is required by law in all 50 states.

Parvovirus: A severe, potentially life-threatening disease that is easily transmitted between dogs. There are four strains of the virus, but it is believed that there is significant "cross-protection" between strains that may be included in individual vaccines.

Distemper: A potentially severe and life-threatening disease with a relatively high risk of exposure, especially in certain regions. In very high-risk distemper environments, young pups may be vaccinated with human measles vaccine, a related virus that offers cross-protection when administered at four to ten weeks of age.

Hepatitis: Caused by canine adenovirus type 1 (CAV-1), but since vaccination with the causative virus has a higher rate of adverse effects, cross-protection is derived from the use of adenovirus type 2 (CAV-2), a cause of respiratory disease and one of the potential causes of canine cough. Vaccination with CAV-2 provides long-term immunity against hepatitis, but relatively less protection against respiratory infection.

Canine cough: Also called tracheobronchitis, actually a fairly complicated result of viral and bacterial offenders; therefore, even with vaccination, protection is incomplete. Wherever dogs congregate, canine cough will likely be spread among them. Intranasal vaccination with *Bordetella* and parainfluenza is the best safeguard, but the duration of immunity does not appear to be very long, typically a year at most. These are non-core vaccines, but vaccination is sometimes mandated by boarding kennels, obedience classes, dog shows and other places where dogs congregate to try to minimize spread of infection.

Leptospirosis: A potentially fatal disease that is more common in some geographic regions. It is capable of being spread to humans. The disease varies with the individual "serovar," or strain, of *Leptospira* involved. Since there does not appear to be much cross-protection between serovars, protection is only as good as the likelihood that the serovar in the vaccine is the same as the one in the pet's local environment. Problems with *Leptospira* vaccines are that protection does not last very long, side effects are not uncommon and a large percentage of dogs (perhaps 30%) may not respond to vaccination. Some Norwich have had bad reactions to this vaccine.

Borrelia burgdorferi: The cause of Lyme disease, the risk of which varies with the geographic area in which the pet lives and travels. Lyme disease is spread by deer ticks in the eastern US and western black-legged ticks in the western part of the country, and the risk of exposure is high in some regions. Lameness, fever and inappetence are most commonly seen in affected dogs. The extent of protection from the vaccine has not been conclusively demonstrated.

Coronavirus: This disease has a high risk of exposure, especially in areas where dogs congregate, but it typically causes only mild to moderate digestive upset (diarrhea, vomiting, etc.). Vaccines are available, but the duration of protection is believed to be relatively short and the effectiveness of the vaccine in preventing infection is considered low.

There are many other vaccinations available, including those for *Giardia* and canine adenovirus-1. While there may be some specific indications for their use, and local risk factors to be considered, they are not widely recommended for most dogs.

INSURANCE

Pet insurance policies are very cost-effective (and very inexpensive by human health-insurance standards), but make sure that you buy the policy long before you intend to use it (preferably starting in puppyhood, because coverage will exclude pre-existing conditions) and that you are actually buying an indemnity insurance plan from an insurance company that is regulated by your state or province. Many insurance policy look-alikes are actually discount clubs that are redeemable only at specific locations and for specific services. An indemnity plan covers your pet at almost all veterinary, specialty and emergency practices and is an excellent way to manage your pet's ongoing healthcare needs.

when your pet needs medical care and you don't want to worry about whether or not you can afford that care.

VACCINATIONS AND INFECTIOUS DISEASES

There has never been an easier time to prevent a variety of infectious diseases in your dog, but the advances we've made in veterinary medicine come with a price—choice. Now while this choice is a good thing, it has never been more difficult for the pet owner (or the veterinarian) to make an informed decision about

the best and safest way to protect pets through vaccination.

Years ago, it was just accepted that puppies got a starter series of vaccinations and then annual "boosters" throughout their lives to keep them protected. As more and more vaccines became available, consumers wanted the convenience of having all of that protection in a single injection. The result was "multivalent" vaccines that crammed a lot of protection into a single syringe. The manufacturers' recommendations were to give the vaccines annually, and this was a simple enough protocol to follow. However, as veterinary medicine has become more sophisticated and we have started looking more at healthcare quandaries rather than convenience, it has become necessary to reevaluate the situation and deal with some tough questions.

It is important to realize that whether or not to use a particular vaccine depends on the risk of contracting the disease against which it protects, the severity of the disease if it is contracted, the duration of immunity provided by the vaccine, the safety of the product and the needs of the individual animal. In a very general sense, rabies, distemper, hepatitis and parvovirus are considered core vaccine needs, while parainfluenza, *Bordetella bronchiseptica*, leptospirosis, coronavirus and borreliosis (Lyme disease) are considered non-core needs and best reserved for animals that demonstrate reasonable risk of contracting the diseases. It is necessary for owners to talk to their vets and make an educated decision regarding the leptospirosis

vaccine for their Norwich, as some have had bad, even fatal, reactions to this vaccine component. Factors such as the area in which you live, the individual dog's genetic background and the potential effectiveness or ineffectiveness of the vaccine are things to consider in determining whether the leptospirosis vaccine is worth giving to your Norwich.

PROBLEM: AND THAT STARTS WITH "P"

Urinary tract problems more commonly affect female dogs, especially those who have been spayed. The first sign that a urinary tract problem exists usually is a strong odor from the urine or an unusual color. Blood in the urine, known as hematuria, is another sign of an infection, related to cystitis, a bladder infection, bladder cancer or a blood-clotting disorder. Urinary tract problems can also be signaled by the dog's straining while urinating, experiencing pain during urination and genital discharge as well as excessive water intake and urination.

Excessive drinking, in and of itself, does not indicate a urinary tract problem. A dog who is drinking more than normal may have a kidney or liver problem, a hormonal disorder or diabetes mellitus. Behaviorists report a disorder known as psychogenic polydipsia, which manifests itself in excessive drinking and urination. If you notice your dog drinking much more than normal, take him to the vet.

NEUTERING/SPAYING

Sterilization procedures (neutering for males/spaying for females) are meant to accomplish several purposes. While the underlying premise is to address the risk of pet overpopulation, there are also some medical and behavioral benefits to the surgeries. For females, spaying prior to the first estrus (heat cycle) leads to a marked reduction in the risk of mammary cancer. There also will be no manifestations of "heat" to attract male dogs and no bleeding in the house. For males, there is prevention of testicular cancer and a reduction in the risk of prostate problems. In both sexes, there may be some limited reduction in aggressive behaviors toward other dogs, and some diminishing of urine marking, roaming and mounting.

While neutering and spaying do indeed prevent animals from contributing to pet overpopulation, even no-cost and low-cost

neutering options have not eliminated the problem. Perhaps one of the main reasons for this is that individuals that intentionally breed their dogs and those that allow their animals to run at large are the main causes of unwanted offspring. Also, animals in shelters are often there because they were abandoned or relinquished, not because they came from unplanned matings. Neutering/spaying is important, but it should be considered in the context of the real causes of animals' ending up in shelters and eventually being euthanized.

One of the important considerations regarding neutering is that it is a surgical procedure. This sometimes gets lost in discussions of low-cost procedures and commoditization of the process. In females, spaying is specifically referred to as an ovariohysterectomy. In this procedure, a midline incision is made in the abdomen and the entire uterus and both ovaries are surgically removed. While this is a major invasive surgical procedure, it usually has few complications, because it is typically performed on healthy young animals. However, it is major surgery, as any woman who has had a hysterectomy will attest.

In males, neutering has traditionally referred to castration, which involves the surgical removal of both testicles. While

still a significant piece of surgery, there is not the abdominal exposure that is required in the female surgery. In addition, there is now a chemical sterilization option, in which a solution is injected into each testicle, leading to atrophy of the sperm-producing cells. This can typically be done under sedation rather than full anesthesia. This is a relatively new approach, and there are no long-term clinical studies yet available.

Neutering/spaying is typically done around six months of age at most veterinary hospitals, although techniques have been pioneered to perform the procedures in animals as young as eight weeks of age. In general, the surgeries on the very young animals are done for the specific reason of sterilizing them before they go to their new homes. This is done in some shelter hospitals for assurance that the animals will definitely not produce any pups. Otherwise, these organizations need to rely on owners to comply with their wishes to have the animals "altered" at a later date, something that does not always happen.

There are some exciting immunocontraceptive "vaccines" currently under development, and there may be a time when contraception in pets will not require surgical procedures. We anxiously await these developments.

S. E. M. BY DR. DENNIS KUNKEL, UNIVERSITY OF HAWAII.

A scanning electron micrograph of a dog flea, Ctenocephalides canis, on dog hair.

EXTERNAL PARASITES

FLEAS

Fleas have been around for millions of years and, while we have better tools now for controlling them than at any time in the past, there still is little chance that they will end up on an endangered species list. Actually, they are very well adapted to living on our pets, and they continue to adapt as we make advances.

The female flea can consume 15 times her weight in blood during active reproduction and can lay as many as 40 eggs a day. These eggs are very resistant to the effects of insecticides. They hatch into larvae, which then mature and spin cocoons. The immature fleas reside in this pupal stage until the time is right for feeding. This pupal stage is also very resistant to the effects of insecticides, and pupae can last in the environment without feeding for many months. Newly emergent fleas are attracted to animals by the warmth of the animals' bodies, movement and exhaled carbon dioxide. However, when they first emerge from their cocoons they orient towards light; thus when an animal passes between a flea and the light source, casting a shadow, the flea pounces and starts to feed. If the animal turns out to be a dog or cat, the reproductive cycle continues. If the flea lands on another type of animal, including a person, the flea will bite but will then look for a more appropriate host. An emerging adult flea can survive without feeding for up to 12 months but, once it tastes blood, it can survive off its host for only three to four days.

It was once thought that fleas spend most of their lives in the environment, but we now know that fleas won't willingly jump off a dog unless leaping to another dog or when physically removed by brushing, bathing or other manipulation. Flea eggs, on the other hand, are shiny and smooth, and they roll off the animal and into the environment. The eggs, larvae and pupae then exist in the environment, but once the adult finds a susceptible animal, it's home sweet home until the flea is forced to seek refuge elsewhere.

Since adult fleas live on the animal and immature forms survive in the environment, a successful treatment plan must address all stages of the flea life cycle. There are now several safe and effective flea-control products that can be applied on a monthly

---

FLEA PREVENTION FOR YOUR DOG

- Discuss with your veterinarian the safest product to protect your dog, likely in the form of a monthly tablet or a liquid preparation placed on the back of the dog's neck.
- For dogs suffering from flea-bite dermatitis, a shampoo or topical insecticide treatment is required.
- Your lawn and property should be sprayed with an insecticide designed to kill fleas and ticks that lurk outdoors.
- Using a flea comb, check the dog's coat regularly for any signs of parasites.
- Practice good housekeeping. Vacuum floors, carpets and furniture regularly, especially in the areas that the dog frequents, and wash the dog's bedding weekly.
- Follow up house-cleaning with carpet shampoos and sprays to rid the house of fleas at all stages of development. Insect growth regulators are the safest option.

---

basis. These include fipronil, imidacloprid, selamectin and permethrin (found in several formulations). Most of these products have significant flea-killing rates within 24 hours. However, none of them will control the immature forms in the environment. To accomplish this, there are a variety of insect growth regulators that can be

THE FLEA'S LIFE CYCLE

What came first, the flea or the egg? This age-old mystery is more difficult to comprehend than the actual cycle of the flea. Fleas usually live only about four months. A female can lay 2,000 eggs in her lifetime.

PHOTO BY CAROLINA BIOLOGICAL SUPPLY CO.

Egg

After ten days of rolling around your carpet or under your furniture, the eggs hatch into larvae, which feed on various and sundry debris. In days or

PHOTO BY CAROLINA BIOLOGICAL SUPPLY CO.

Larva

months, depending on the climate, the larvae spin cocoons and develop into the pupal or nymph stage, which quickly develop into fleas.

Pupa

These immature fleas must locate a host within 10 to 14 days or they will die. Only about 1% of the flea population exist as adult fleas, while the other 99% exist as eggs, larvae or pupae.

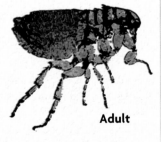

Adult

KILL FLEAS THE NATURAL WAY

If you choose not to go the route of conventional medication, there are some natural ways to ward off fleas:

- Dust your dog with a natural flea powder, composed of such herbal goodies as rosemary, wormwood, pennyroyal, citronella, rue, tobacco powder and eucalyptus.
- Apply diatomaceous earth, the fossilized remains of single-cell algae, to your carpets, furniture and pet's bedding. Even though it's not good for dogs, it's even worse for fleas, which will dry up swiftly and die.
- Brush your dog frequently, give him adequate exercise and let him fast occasionally. All of these activities strengthen the dog's system and make him more resistant to disease and parasites.
- Bathe your dog with a capful of pennyroyal or eucalyptus oil.
- Feed a natural diet, free of additives and preservatives. Add some fresh garlic and brewer's yeast to the dog's morning portion, as these items have flea-repelling properties.

sprayed into the environment (e.g., pyriproxyfen, methoprene, fenoxycarb) as well as insect development inhibitors such as lufenuron that can be administered. These compounds have no effect on adult fleas, but they stop immature forms from developing into adults. In years gone by, we relied heavily on toxic insecticides (such as organophosphates, organochlorines and carbamates) to manage the flea problem, but today's options are not only much safer to use on our pets but also safer for the environment.

TICKS

Ticks are members of the spider class (arachnids) and are blood-sucking parasites capable of transmitting a variety of diseases, including Lyme disease, ehrlichiosis, babesiosis and Rocky Mountain spotted fever. It's easy to see ticks on your own skin, but it is more of a challenge when your furry companion is affected. Whenever you happen to be planning a stroll in a tick-infested area (especially forests, grassy or wooded areas or parks) be prepared to do a thorough inspection of your dog afterward to search for ticks. Ticks can be tricky, so make sure you spend time looking in the ears, between the toes and everywhere else where a tick might hide. Ticks need to be attached for 24–72 hours before they transmit most of the diseases that they carry, so you do have a window of opportunity for some preventive intervention.

A TICKING BOMB

There is nothing good about a tick's harpooning his nose into your dog's skin. Among the diseases caused by ticks are Rocky Mountain spotted fever, canine ehrlichiosis, canine babesiosis, canine hepatozoonosis and Lyme disease. If a dog is allergic to the saliva of a female wood tick, he can develop tick paralysis.

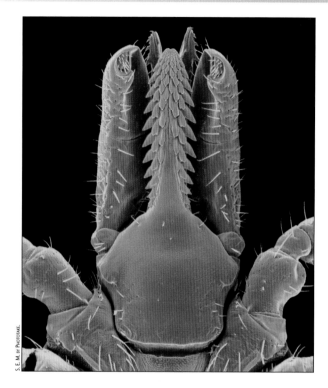

S. E. M. BY PHOTOTAKE.

A scanning electron micrograph of the head of a female deer tick, *Ixodes dammini,* a parasitic tick that carries Lyme disease.

Female ticks live to eat and breed. They can lay between 4,000 and 5,000 eggs and they die soon after. Males, on the other hand, live only to mate with the females and continue the process as long as they are able. Most ticks live on multiple hosts before parasitizing dogs. The immature forms typically reside on grass and shrubs, waiting for susceptible animals to walk by. The larvae and nymph stages typically feed on wildlife.

If only a few ticks are present on a dog, they can be plucked out, but it is important to remove the entire head and mouthparts,

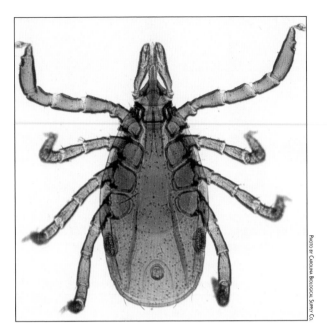

PHOTO BY CAROLINA BIOLOGICAL SUPPLY CO.

Deer tick,
Ixodes dammini.

which may be deeply embedded in the skin. This is best accomplished with forceps designed especially for this purpose; fingers can be used but should be protected with rubber gloves, plastic wrap or at least a paper towel. The tick should be grasped as closely as possible to the animal's skin and should be pulled upward with steady, even pressure. Do not squeeze, crush or puncture the body of the tick or you risk exposure to any disease carried by that tick. Once the ticks have been removed, the sites of attachment should be disinfected. Your hands should then be washed with soap and water to further minimize risk of contagion. The tick should be

disposed of in a container of alcohol or household bleach.

Some of the newer flea products, specifically those with fipronil, selamectin and permethrin, have effect against some, but not all, species of tick. Flea collars containing appropriate pesticides (e.g., propoxur, chlorfen-vinphos) can aid in tick control. In most areas, such collars should be placed on animals in March, at the beginning of the tick season, and changed regularly. Leaving the collar on when the pesticide level is waning invites the development of resistance. Amitraz collars are also used for tick control, and the active ingredient does not interfere with other flea-control products. The ingredient helps prevent the attachment of ticks to the skin and will cause those ticks already on the skin to detach themselves.

TICK CONTROL

Removal of underbrush and leaf litter and the thinning of trees in areas where tick control is desired are recommended. These actions remove the cover and food sources for small animals that serve as hosts for ticks. With continued mowing of grasses in these areas, the probability of ticks' surviving is further reduced. A variety of insecticide ingredients (e.g., resmethrin, carbaryl, permethrin, chlorpyrifos, dioxathion and allethrin) are registered for tick control around the home.

Mites

Mites are tiny arachnid parasites that parasitize the skin of dogs. Skin diseases caused by mites are referred to as "mange," and there are many different forms seen in dogs. These forms are very different from one another, each one warranting an individual description.

Sarcoptic mange, or scabies, is one of the itchiest conditions that affects dogs. The microscopic *Sarcoptes* mites burrow into the superficial layers of the skin and can drive dogs crazy with itchiness. They are also communicable to people, although they can't complete their reproductive cycle on people. In addition to being tiny, the mites also are often difficult to find when trying to make a diagnosis. Skin scrapings from multiple areas are examined microscopically but, even then, sometimes the mites cannot be found.

Fortunately, scabies is relatively easy to treat, and there are a variety of products that will successfully kill the mites. Since the mites can't live in the environment for very long without feeding, a complete cure is usually possible within four to eight weeks.

Cheyletiellosis is caused by a relatively large mite, which sometimes can be seen even without a microscope. Often referred to as "walking dandruff," this also causes itching, but not usually as profound as with scabies.

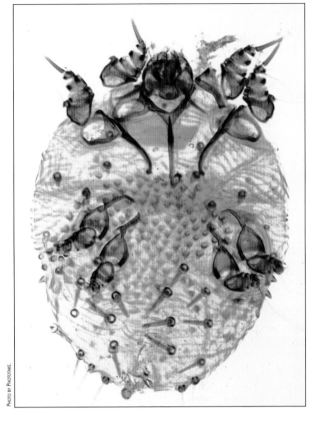

Photo by Phototake.

While *Cheyletiella* mites can survive somewhat longer in the environment than scabies mites, they too are relatively easy to treat, being responsive to not only the medications used to treat scabies but also often to flea-control products.

Otodectes cynotis is the canine ear mite and is one of the more common causes of mange, especially in young dogs in shelters or pet stores. That's because the mites are typically present in large numbers and are quickly spread to

Sarcoptes scabiei, commonly known as the "itch mite."

Micrograph of a dog louse, *Heterodoxus spiniger.* Female lice attach their eggs to the hairs of the dog. As the eggs hatch, the larval lice bite and feed on the blood. Lice can also feed on dead skin and hair. This feeding activity can cause hair loss and skin problems.

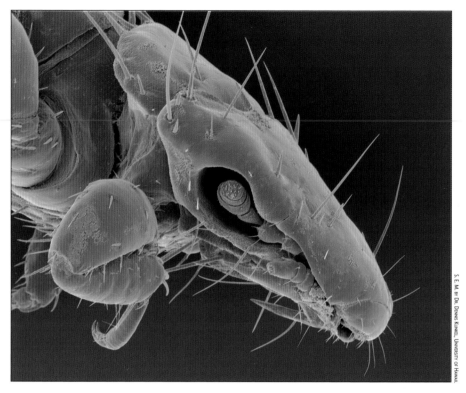

S. E. M. by Dr. Dennis Kunkel, University of Hawaii

nearby animals. The mites rarely do much harm but can be difficult to eradicate if the treatment regimen is not comprehensive. While many try to treat the condition with ear drops only, this is the most common cause of treatment failure. Ear drops cause the mites to simply move out of the ears and as far away as possible (usually to the base of the tail) until the insecticide levels in the ears drop to an acceptable level—then it's back to business as usual! The successful treatment of ear mites requires treating all animals in the household with a systemic insecticide, such as selamectin, or a combination of miticidal ear drops combined with whole-body flea-control preparations.

Demodicosis, sometimes referred to as red mange, can be one of the most difficult forms of mange to treat. Part of the problem has to do with the fact that the mites live in the hair follicles and they are relatively well shielded from topical and systemic products. The main issue, however, is that demodectic mange typically results only when there is some underlying process interfering with the dog's immune system.

Since *Demodex* mites are

normal residents of the skin of mammals, including humans, there is usually a mite population explosion only when the immune system fails to keep the number of mites in check. In young animals, the immune deficit may be transient or may reflect an actual inherited immune problem. In older animals, demodicosis is usually seen only when there is another disease hampering the immune system, such as diabetes, cancer, thyroid problems or the use of immune-suppressing drugs. Accordingly, treatment involves not only trying to kill the mange mites but also discerning what is interfering with immune function and correcting it if possible.

Chiggers represent several different species of mite that don't parasitize dogs specifically, but do latch on to passersby and can cause irritation. The problem is most prevalent in wooded areas in the late summer and fall. Treatment is not difficult, as the mites do not complete their life cycle on dogs and are susceptible to a variety of miticidal products.

ILLUSTRATION BY PHOTOTAKE

Illustration of Demodex folliculoram.

MOSQUITOES
Mosquitoes have long been known to transmit a variety of diseases to people, as well as just being biting pests during warm weather. They also pose a real risk to pets. Not only do they carry deadly heartworms but recently there also has been much concern over their involvement with West Nile virus. While we can avoid heartworm with the use of preventive medications, there are no such preventives for West Nile virus. The only method of prevention in endemic areas is active mosquito control. Fortunately, most dogs that have been exposed to the virus only developed flu-like symptoms and, to date, there have not been the large number of reported deaths in canines as seen in some other species.

MOSQUITO REPELLENT
Low concentrations of DEET (less than 10%), found in many human mosquito repellents, have been safely used in dogs but, in these concentrations, probably give only about two hours of protection. DEET may be safe in these small concentrations, but since it is not licensed for use on dogs, there is no research proving its safety for dogs. Products containing permethrin give the longest-lasting protection, perhaps two to four weeks. As DEET is not licensed for use on dogs, and both DEET and permethrin can be quite toxic to cats, appropriate care should be exercised. Other products, such as those containing oil of citronella, also have some mosquito-repellent activity, but typically have a relatively short duration of action.

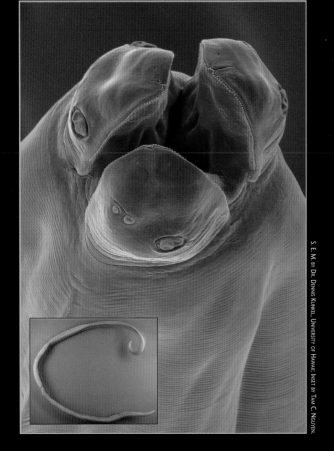

ASCARID DANGERS

The most commonly encountered worms in dogs are roundworms known as ascarids. *Toxascaris leonine* and *Toxocara canis* are the two species that infect dogs. Subsisting in the dog's stomach and intestines, adult roundworms can grow to 7 inches in length and adult females can lay in excess of 200,000 eggs in a single day.

In humans, visceral larval migrans affects people who have ingested eggs of *Toxocara canis*, which frequently contaminates children's sandboxes, beaches and park grounds. The roundworms reside in the human's stomach and intestines, as they would in a dog's, but do not mature. Instead, they find their way to the liver, lungs and skin, or even to the heart or kidneys in severe cases. Deworming puppies is critical in preventing the infection in humans, and young children should never handle nursing pups who have not been dewormed.

The ascarid roundworm **Toxocara canis,** *showing the mouth with three lips.* **INSET:** *Photomicrograph of the roundworm* **Ascaris lumbricoides.**

INTERNAL PARASITES: WORMS

ASCARIDS

Ascarids are intestinal roundworms that rarely cause severe disease in dogs. Nonetheless, they are of major public health significance because they can be transferred to people. Sadly, it is children who are most commonly affected by the parasite, probably from inadvertently ingesting ascarid-contaminated soil. In fact, many yards and children's sandboxes contain appreciable numbers of ascarid eggs. So, while ascarids don't bite dogs or latch onto their intestines to suck blood, they do cause some nasty medical conditions in children and are best eradicated from our furry friends. Because pups can start passing ascarid eggs by three weeks of age, most parasite-control programs begin at two weeks of age and are repeated every two weeks until pups are eight weeks old. It is important to

HOOKED ON ANCYLOSTOMA

Adult dogs can become infected by the bloodsucking nematodes we commonly call hookworms via ingesting larvae from the ground or via the larvae penetrating the dog's skin. It is not uncommon for infected dogs to show no symptoms of hookworm infestation. Sometimes symptoms occur within ten days of exposure. These symptoms can include bloody diarrhea, anemia, loss of weight and general weakness. Dogs pass the hookworm eggs in their stools, which serves as the vet's method of identifying the infestation. The hookworm larvae can encyst themselves in the dog's tissues and be released when the dog is experiencing stress.

Caused by an *Ancylostoma* species whose common host is the dog, cutaneous larval migrans affects humans, causing itching and lumps and streaks beneath the surface of the skin.

S. E. M. BY DR. DENNIS KUNKEL, UNIVERSITY OF HAWAII.

realize that bitches can pass ascarids to their pups even if they test negative prior to whelping. Accordingly, bitches are best treated at the same time as the pups.

HOOKWORMS

Unlike ascarids, hookworms do latch onto a dog's intestinal tract and can cause significant loss of blood and protein. Similar to ascarids, hookworms can be transmitted to humans, where they cause a condition known as cutaneous larval migrans. Dogs can become infected either by consuming the infective larvae or by the larvae's penetrating the skin directly. People most often get infected when they are lying on the ground (such as on a beach) and the larvae penetrate the skin. Yes, the larvae can penetrate through a beach blanket. Hookworms are typically suscep-tible to the same medications used to treat ascarids.

The hookworm *Ancylostoma caninum* infests the intestines of dogs. INSET: Note the row of hooks at the posterior end, used to anchor the worm to the intestinal wall.

WHIPWORMS

Whipworms latch onto the lower aspects of the dog's colon and can cause cramping and diarrhea. Eggs do not start to appear in the dog's feces until about three months after the dog was infected. This worm has a peculiar life cycle, which makes it more difficult to control than ascarids or hookworms. The good thing is that whipworms rarely are transferred to people.

Some of the medications used to treat ascarids and hookworms are also effective against whipworms, but, in general, a separate treatment protocol is needed. Since most of the medications are effective against the adults but not the eggs or larvae, treatment is typically repeated in three weeks, and then often in three

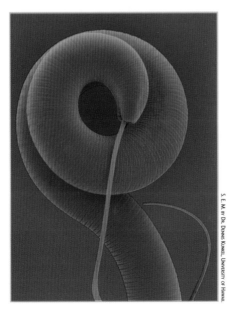

Adult whipworm, *Trichuris* sp., an intestinal parasite.

S. E. M. BY DR. DENNIS KUNKEL, UNIVERSITY OF HAWAII.

WORM-CONTROL GUIDELINES

- Practice sanitary habits with your dog and home.
- Clean up after your dog and don't let him sniff or eat other dogs' droppings.
- Control insects and fleas in the dog's environment. Fleas, lice, cockroaches, beetles, mice and rats can act as hosts for various worms.
- Prevent dogs from eating uncooked meat, raw poultry and dead animals.
- Keep dogs and children from playing in sand and soil.
- Kennel dogs on cement or gravel; avoid dirt runs.
- Administer heartworm preventives regularly.
- Have your vet examine your dog's stools at your annual visits.
- Select a boarding kennel carefully so as to avoid contamination from other dogs or an unsanitary environment.
- Prevent dogs from roaming. Obey local leash laws.

months as well. Unfortunately, since dogs don't develop resistance to whipworms, it is difficult to prevent them from getting reinfected if they visit soil contaminated with whipworm eggs.

TAPEWORMS

There are many different species of tapeworm that affect dogs, but *Dipylidium caninum* is probably the most common and is spread by fleas. Flea larvae feed on organic debris and tapeworm eggs in the environment and, when a dog chews at himself and manages to ingest fleas, he might get a dose of tapeworm at the same time. The tapeworm then develops further in the intestine of the dog.

The tapeworm itself, which is a parasitic flatworm that latches onto the intestinal wall, is composed of numerous segments. When the segments break off into the intestine (as proglottids), they may accumulate around the rectum, like grains of rice. While this tapeworm is disgusting in its behavior, it is not directly communicable to humans (although humans can also get infected by swallowing fleas).

A much more dangerous flatworm is *Echinococcus multilocularis*, which is typically found in foxes, coyotes and wolves. The eggs are passed in the feces and infect rodents, and, when dogs eat the rodents, the dogs can be infected by thousands of adult tapeworms. While the parasites don't cause many problems in dogs, this is considered the most lethal worm infection that people can get. Take appropriate precautions if you live in an area in which these tapeworms are found. Do not use mulch that may contain feces of dogs, cats or wildlife, and

discourage your pets from hunting wildlife. Treat these tapeworm infections aggressively in pets, because if humans get infected, approximately half die.

HEARTWORMS

Heartworm disease is caused by the parasite *Dirofilaria immitis* and is seen in dogs around the world. A member of the roundworm group, it is spread between dogs by the bite of an infected mosquito. The mosquito injects infective larvae into the dog's skin with its bite, and these larvae develop under the skin for a period of time before making their way to the heart. There they develop into adults, which grow and create blockages of the heart, lungs and major blood vessels there. They also start producing offspring (microfilariae)

A dog tapeworm proglottid (body segment).

The dog tapeworm *Taenia pisiformis*.

S. E. M. by Dr. Dennis Kunkel, University of Hawaii

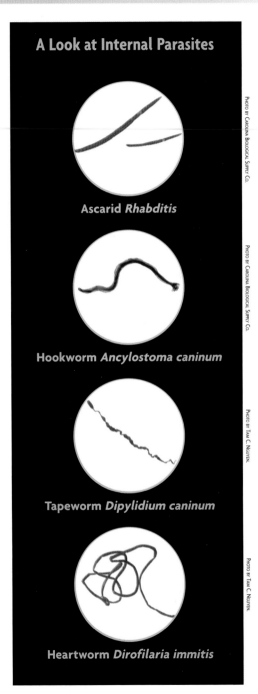

A Look at Internal Parasites

Ascarid *Rhabditis*

Hookworm *Ancylostoma caninum*

Tapeworm *Dipylidium caninum*

Heartworm *Dirofilaria immitis*

PHOTO BY CAROLINA BIOLOGICAL SUPPLY CO.

PHOTO BY CAROLINA BIOLOGICAL SUPPLY CO.

PHOTO BY TAM C. NGUYEN.

PHOTO BY TAM C. NGUYEN.

and these microfilariae circulate in the bloodstream, waiting to hitch a ride when the next mosquito bites. Once in the mosquito, the microfilariae develop into infective larvae and the entire process is repeated.

When dogs get infected with heartworm, over time they tend to develop symptoms associated with heart disease, such as coughing, exercise intolerance and potentially many other manifestations. Diagnosis is confirmed by either seeing the microfilariae themselves in blood samples or using immunologic tests (antigen testing) to identify the presence of adult heartworms. Since antigen tests measure the presence of adult heartworms and microfilarial tests measure offspring produced by adults, neither are positive until six to seven months after the initial infection. However, the beginning of damage can occur by fifth-stage larvae as early as three months after infection. Thus it is possible for dogs to be harboring problem-causing larvae for up to three months before either type of test would identify an infection.

The good news is that there are great protocols available for preventing heartworm in dogs. Testing is critical in the process, and it is important to understand the benefits as well as the limitations of such testing. All dogs six months of age or older that have not been on continuous heartworm-preventive medication should be

Life Cycle of the Heartworm

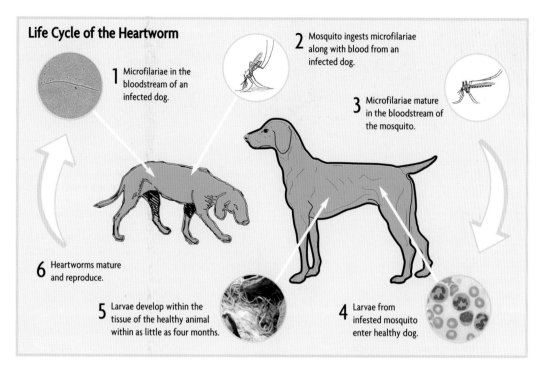

1 Microfilariae in the bloodstream of an infected dog.

2 Mosquito ingests microfilariae along with blood from an infected dog.

3 Microfilariae mature in the bloodstream of the mosquito.

4 Larvae from infested mosquito enter healthy dog.

5 Larvae develop within the tissue of the healthy animal within as little as four months.

6 Heartworms mature and reproduce.

screened with microfilarial or antigen tests. For dogs receiving preventive medication, periodic antigen testing helps assess the effectiveness of the preventives. The American Heartworm Society guidelines suggest that annual retesting may not be necessary when owners have absolutely provided continuous heartworm prevention. Retesting on a two- to three-year interval may be sufficient in these cases. However, your veterinarian will likely have specific guidelines under which heartworm preventives will be prescribed, and many prefer to err on the side of safety and retest annually.

It is indeed fortunate that heartworm is relatively easy to prevent, because treatments can be as life-threatening as the disease itself. Treatment requires a two-step process that kills the adult heartworms first and then the microfilariae. Prevention is obviously preferable; this involves a once-monthly oral or topical treatment. The most common oral preventives include ivermectin (not suitable for some breeds), moxidectin and milbemycin oxime; the once-a-month topical drug selamectin provides heartworm protection in addition to flea, tick and other parasite controls.

THE **ABC**s OF
Emergency Care

Abrasions
Clean wound with running water or 3% hydrogen peroxide. Pat dry with gauze and spray with antibiotic. Do not cover.

Animal Bites
Clean area with soap and saline solution or water. Apply pressure to any bleeding area. Apply antibiotic ointment.

Antifreeze Poisoning
Induce vomiting and take dog to the vet.

Bee Sting
Remove stinger and apply soothing lotion or cold compress; give antihistamine in proper dosage.

Bleeding
Apply pressure directly to wound with gauze or towel for five to ten minutes. If wound does not stop bleeding, wrap wound with gauze and adhesive tape.

Bloat/Gastric Torsion
Immediately take the dog to the vet or emergency clinic; phone from car. No time to waste.

Burns
Chemical: Bathe dog with water and pet shampoo. Rinse in saline solution. Apply antibiotic ointment.

Acid: Rinse with water. Apply one part baking soda, two parts water to affected area.

Alkali: Rinse with water. Apply one part vinegar, four parts water to affected area.

Electrical: Apply antibiotic ointment. Seek veterinary assistance immediately.

Choking
If the dog is on the verge of collapsing, wedge a solid object, such as the handle of screwdriver, between molars on one side of the mouth to keep mouth open. Pull tongue out. Use long-nosed pliers or fingers to remove foreign object. Do not push the object down the dog's throat. For small or medium dogs, hold dog upside down by hind legs and shake firmly to dislodge foreign object.

Chlorine Ingestion
With clean water, rinse the mouth and eyes. Give the dog water to drink; contact the vet.

Constipation
Feed dog 2 tablespoons bran flakes with each meal. Encourage drinking water. Mix ¼ teaspoon mineral oil in dog's food.

Diarrhea
Withhold food for 12 to 24 hours. Feed dog anti-diarrheal with eyedropper. When feeding resumes, feed one part boiled hamburger, one part plain cooked rice, ¼ to ¾ cup four times daily.

Dog Bite
Snip away hair around puncture wound; clean with 3% hydrogen peroxide; apply tincture of iodine. If wound appears deep, take the dog to the vet.

Frostbite
Wrap the dog in a heavy blanket. Warm affected area with a warm bath for ten minutes. Red color to skin will return with circulation; if tissues are pale after 20 minutes, contact the vet.

Use a portable, durable container large enough to contain all items

Heat Stroke
Partially submerge the dog in cold water; if no response within ten minutes, contact the vet.

Hot Spots
Mix 2 packets Domeboro® with 2 cups water. Saturate cloth with mixture and apply to hot spots for 15 to 30 minutes. Apply antibiotic ointment. Repeat every six to eight hours.

Poisonous Plants
Wash affected area with soap and water. Cleanse with alcohol. For foxtail/grass, apply antibiotic ointment.

Rat Poison Ingestion
Induce vomiting. Keep dog calm, maintain dog's normal body temperature (use blanket or heating pad). Get to the vet for antidote.

Shock
Keep the dog calm and warm; call for veterinary assistance.

Snake Bite
If possible, bandage the area and apply pressure. If the area is not conducive to bandaging, use ice to control bleeding. Get immediate help from the vet.

Tick Removal
Apply flea and tick spray directly on tick. Wait one minute. Using tweezers or wearing plastic gloves, apply constant pull while grasping tick's body. Apply antibiotic ointment.

Vomiting
Restrict dog's water intake; offer a few ice cubes. Withhold food for next meal. Contact vet if vomiting persists longer than 24 hours.

DOG OWNER'S FIRST-AID KIT
❑ **Gauze bandages/swabs**
❑ **Adhesive and non-adhesive bandages**
❑ **Antibiotic powder**
❑ **Antiseptic wash**
❑ **Hydrogen peroxide 3%**
❑ **Antibiotic ointment**
❑ **Lubricating jelly**
❑ **Rectal thermometer**
❑ **Nylon muzzle**
❑ **Scissors and forceps**
❑ **Eyedropper**
❑ **Syringe**
❑ **Anti-bacterial/fungal solution**
❑ **Saline solution**
❑ **Antihistamine**
❑ **Cotton balls**
❑ **Nail clippers**
❑ **Screwdriver/pen knife**
❑ **Flashlight**
❑ **Emergency phone numbers**

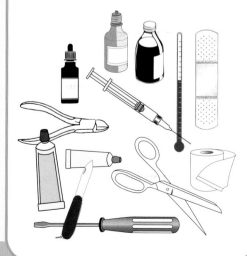

NORWICH TERRIER

When we bring home a puppy, full of the energy and exuberance that accompanies youth, we hope for a long, happy and fulfilling relationship with the new family member. Even when we adopt an older dog, we look forward to the years of companionship ahead with a new canine friend. However, aging is inevitable for all creatures, and there will come a time when your Norwich Terrier reaches his senior years and will need special considerations and attention to his care.

WHEN IS MY DOG A "SENIOR"?

In general, pure-bred dogs are considered to have achieved senior status when they reach 75% of their breed's average lifespan. Norwich owners are among the most fortunate when it comes to the longevity of their breed. Healthy, well-cared-for Norwich Terriers are blessed with average lifespans of 12–15 years, sometimes longer.

Obviously, the old "seven dog years to one human year" theory is not exact. In puppyhood, a dog's year is actually comparable to more than seven human years, considering the puppy's rapid growth during his first year. Then, in adulthood, the ratio decreases. Regardless, the more viable rule of thumb is that the larger the dog, the shorter his expected lifespan. Of course, this can vary among individual dogs, with many living longer than expected, which we hope is the case!

WHAT ARE THE SIGNS?

By the time your dog has reached his senior years, you will know him very well, so the physical and behavioral changes that accompany aging should be noticeable to you. Humans and dogs share the most obvious physical sign of aging: gray hair! Graying often occurs first on the muzzle and face, around the eyes. Other telltale signs are the dog's overall decrease in activity. Your older dog might be more content to nap and rest, and he may not show the same old enthusiasm when it's time to play in the yard or go for a walk. Other physical signs include significant weight loss or gain; more labored movement; skin and coat problems, possibly hair loss; sight and/or hearing problems; changes in toileting habits, perhaps seeming "unhousebroken" at times; and tooth decay, bad breath or other mouth problems.

There are behavioral changes that go along with aging, too. There

ADAPTING TO AGE

As dogs age and their once-keen senses begin to deteriorate, they can experience stress and confusion. However, dogs are very adaptable, and most can adjust to deficiencies in their sight and hearing. As these processes often deteriorate gradually, the dog makes adjustments gradually, too. Because dogs become so familiar with the layout of their homes and yards, and with their daily routines, they are able to get around even if they cannot see or hear as well. Help your senior dog by keeping things consistent around the house. Keep up with your regular times for walking and potty trips, and do not relocate his crate or rearrange the furniture; keep a safe environment for him by "accident-proofing." Your dog is a very adaptable creature and can make compensation for his diminished ability, but you want to help him along the way and not make changes that will cause him confusion.

are numerous causes for behavioral changes. Sometimes a dog's apparent confusion results from a physical change like diminished sight or hearing. If his confusion causes him to be afraid, he may act aggressively or defensively. He may sleep more frequently because his daily walks, though shorter now, tire him out. He may begin to experience separation anxiety or, conversely, become less interested in petting and attention.

There also are clinical conditions that cause behavioral changes in older dogs. One such condition is known as canine cognitive dysfunction (familiarly known as "old-dog" syndrome). It can be frustrating for an owner whose dog is affected with cognitive dysfunction, as it can result in behavioral changes of all types, most seemingly unexplainable. Common changes include the dog's forgetting aspects of the daily routine, such as times to eat, go out for walks, relieve himself and the like. Along the same lines, you may take your dog out at the regular time for a potty trip and he may have no idea why he is there. Sometimes a placid dog will begin to show aggressive or possessive tendencies or, conversely, a hyperactive dog will start to "mellow out."

Disease also can be the cause of behavioral changes in senior dogs. Hormonal problems (Cushing's disease is common in older dogs), diabetes and thyroid disease can cause increased appetite, which can lead to aggression related to food guarding. It's better to be proactive with your dog as he gets older, making more frequent trips to the vet if necessary and having bloodwork done to test for the diseases that can commonly befall older dogs *before* they happen.

This is not to say that, as dogs age, they all fall apart physically and become nasty in personality.

RUBDOWN REMEDY

A good remedy for an aching dog is to give him a gentle massage each day, or even a few times a day if possible. This can be especially beneficial before your dog gets out of his bed in the morning. Just as in humans, massage can decrease pain in dogs, whether the dog is arthritic or just afflicted by the stiffness that accompanies old age. Gently massage his joints and limbs, as well as petting him on his entire body. This can help his circulation and flexibility and ease any joint or muscle aches. Massaging your dog has benefits for you, too; in fact, just petting our dogs can cause reduced levels of stress and lower our blood pressure. Massage and petting also help you find any previously undetected lumps, bumps or abnormalities. Often these are not visible and only turn up by being felt.

Investigate new dietary supplements made for arthritic dogs. Studies have found that products containing glucosamine added once or twice daily to the senior dog's food can have beneficial effects on the dog's joints. Many of these products also contain natural anti-inflammatories such as chondroitin, MSM and cetyl myristoleate, as well as natural herbal remedies and nutmeg. Talk to your vet about these supplements.

The aforementioned changes are discussed to alert owners to the things that may happen as their dogs get older. Many hardy dogs remain active and alert well into old age. However, it can be frustrating and heartbreaking for owners to see their beloved dogs change physically and temperamentally. Just know that it's the same Norwich Terrier under there, and that he still loves you and appreciates your care, which he needs now more than ever.

CARING FOR MY AGING DOG

Every dog is an individual in terms of aging. Even if your dog shows no outward signs of aging, he should begin a senior-care program at the age recommended by your vet. Although we've used the "75% rule" to determine a Norwich's senior status, your vet may suggest healthcare changes earlier in the dog's life. He may not show it, but he's not a pup anymore! By providing him with extra attention to his veterinary care, you will be practicing good preventive medicine, ensuring that the rest of your dog's life will be as long, active, happy and healthy as possible. If you do notice indications of aging, such as graying and/or changes in sleeping, eating or toileting habits, this is a sign to set up a senior-care visit with your vet right away to make sure that these changes are not related to any health problems.

To start, senior dogs should visit the vet twice yearly for exams, routine tests and overall evaluations. Many veterinarians have special screening programs especially for senior dogs that can include a thorough physical exam; blood test to determine complete blood count; serum biochemistry test, which screens for liver, kidney and blood problems as well as cancer; urinalysis; and dental exams. With these tests, it can be determined whether your dog has any health problems; the results also establish a baseline for your pet against which future test results can be compared.

In addition to these tests, your vet may suggest additional testing, including an EKG, tests for glaucoma and other problems of the eye, chest x-rays, screening for tumors, blood pressure test, test for thyroid function and screening for parasites and reassessment of his preventive program. Your vet also will ask you questions about your dog's diet and activity level, what you feed and the amounts that you feed. This information, along with his evaluation of the dog's overall condition, will enable him to suggest proper dietary changes, if needed.

This may seem like quite a work-up for your pet, but veterinarians advise that older dogs need more frequent attention so that any health problems can be detected as early as possible. Serious conditions like kidney disease, heart disease and cancer may not present outward symptoms, or the problem may go undetected if the symptoms are mistaken by owners as just part of the aging process.

There are some conditions more common in elderly dogs that are difficult to ignore. Cognitive dysfunction shares much in common with senility and Alzheimer's disease, and dogs are not immune. Dogs can become confused and/or disoriented, lose their house-training, have abnormal sleep-wake cycles and interact differently with their owners. Be heartened by the fact that, in some ways, there are more treatment options for dogs with cognitive dysfunction than for people with similar conditions. There is good evidence that continued stimulation

---

WEATHER WORRIES

Older pets are less tolerant of extremes in weather, both heat and cold. Your older dog should not spend extended periods in the sun; when outdoors in the warm weather, make sure he does not become overheated. In chilly weather, consider a sweater for your dog when outdoors and limit time spent outside. Whether or not his coat is thinning, he will need provisions to keep him warm when the weather is cold. You may even place his bed by a heating duct in your living room or bedroom.

in the form of games, play, training and exercise can help to maintain cognitive function. There are also medications (such as seligiline) and antioxidant-fortified senior diets that have been shown to be very beneficial.

Cancer is also a condition more common in the elderly. Almost all of the cancers seen in people are also seen in pets. Even lung cancer, which is a major killer in humans, can affect dogs who are exposed to second-hand smoke. If pets are getting regular physical examinations, cancers are often detected early. There are a variety of cancer therapies available today, and many pets continue to live happy lives with appropriate treatment.

Degenerative joint disease, often referred to as arthritis, is another malady common to both elderly dogs and humans. A lifetime of wear and tear on joints and running around at play eventually takes its toll and results in stiffness and difficulty in getting around. As dogs live longer and healthier lives, it is natural that they should eventually feel some of the effects of aging. Once again, if your Norwich has been getting regular veterinary care, your pet should not have been carrying extra pounds all those years and wearing those joints out before their time. If your pet was unfortunate enough to inherit hip dysplasia, osteochondritis dissecans or any of the other developmental orthopedic diseases, battling the onset of degenerative joint disease was probably a longstanding goal. In any case, there are now many effective remedies for managing degenerative joint disease and a number of remarkable surgeries as well.

Aside from the extra veterinary care, there is much you can do at home to keep your older dog in good condition. The dog's diet is an important factor. If your dog's appetite decreases, he will not be

COPING WITH A BLIND DOG
Blindness is one of the unfortunate realities of growing old, for both dogs and humans. Owners of blind dogs should not give up hope, as most dogs adapt to their compromised state with grace and patience. A sudden loss of sight poses more stress on the dog than a gradual loss, such as that through cataracts. Some dogs may need your assistance to help them get around; others will move around seemingly uninhibited. Owners may need to retrain the dog to handle some basic tasks. Teaching commands like "Wait," "Stop" and "Slow" are handy as you help the dog learn to maneuver around his world. You are now more than the team captain, you're the coach and cheerleader! If your blind dog is showing signs of depression, it is your job to encourage him and give him moral support, just as you might for a member of your family or a good friend.

Number-One Killer Disease in Dogs: CANCER

In every age, there is a word associated with a disease or plague that causes humans to shudder. In the 21st century, that word is "cancer." Just as cancer is the leading cause of death in humans, it claims nearly half the lives of dogs that die from a natural disease as well as half the dogs that die over the age of ten years.

Described as a genetic disease, cancer becomes a greater risk as the dog ages. Vets and dog owners have become increasingly aware of the threat of cancer to dogs. Statistics reveal that one dog in every five will develop cancer, the most common of which is skin cancer. Many cancers, including prostate, ovarian and breast cancer, can be avoided by spaying and neutering our dogs by the age of six months.

Early detection of cancer can save or extend a dog's life, so it is absolutely vital for owners to have their dogs examined by a qualified vet or oncologist immediately upon detection of any abnormality. Certain dietary guidelines have also proven to reduce the onset and spread of cancer. Foods based on fish rather than beef, due to the presence of Omega-3 fatty acids, are recommended. Other amino acids such as glutamine have significant benefits for canines, particularly those breeds that show a greater susceptibility to cancer.

Cancer management and treatments promise hope for future generations of canines. Since the disease is genetic, breeders should never breed a dog whose parents, grandparents and any related siblings have developed cancer. It is difficult to know whether to exclude an otherwise healthy dog from a breeding program, as the disease udually does not manifest itself until the dog's senior years.

RECOGNIZE CANCER WARNING SIGNS

Since early detection can possibly rescue your dog from becoming a cancer statistic, it is essential for owners to recognize the possible signs and seek the assistance of a qualified professional.

- Abnormal bumps or lumps that continue to grow
- Bleeding or discharge from any body cavity
- Persistent stiffness or lameness
- Recurrent sores or sores that do not heal
- Inappetence
- Breathing difficulties
- Weight loss
- Bad breath or odors
- General malaise and fatigue
- Eating and swallowing problems
- Difficulty urinating and defecating

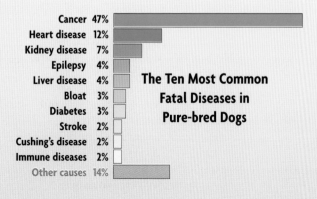

Cancer	47%
Heart disease	12%
Kidney disease	7%
Epilepsy	4%
Liver disease	4%
Bloat	3%
Diabetes	3%
Stroke	2%
Cushing's disease	2%
Immune diseases	2%
Other causes	14%

The Ten Most Common Fatal Diseases in Pure-bred Dogs

getting the nutrients he needs. He also will lose weight, which is unhealthy for a dog at a proper weight. Conversely, an older dog's metabolism is slower and he usually exercises less, but he should not be allowed to become obese. Obesity in an older dog is especially risky, because extra pounds mean extra stress on the body, increasing his vulnerability to heart disease. Additionally, the extra pounds make it harder for the dog to move about.

You should discuss age-related feeding changes with your vet. For a dog who has lost interest in food, it may be suggested to try some different types of food until you find something new that the dog likes. For an obese dog, a "light"- formula dog food or reducing food portions may be advised, along with exercise appropriate to his physical condition and energy level.

As for exercise, the senior dog should not be allowed to become a "couch potato" despite his old age. He may not be able to handle the morning run, long walks and vigorous games of fetch, but he still needs to get up and get moving. Keep up with your daily walks, but keep the distances shorter and let your dog set the pace. If he gets to the point where he's not up for walks, let him stroll around the yard. On the other hand, many dogs remain very active in their senior years, so base changes to the exercise program on your own individual dog and what he's capable of. Don't worry, your Norwich Terrier will let you know when it's time to rest.

Keep up with your grooming routine as you always have. Be extra-diligent about checking the skin and coat for problems. Older dogs can experience thinning coats as a normal aging process, but they can also lose hair as a result of medical problems. Some thinning is normal, but patches of baldness or the loss of significant amounts of hair is not.

Hopefully, you've been regular with brushing your dog's teeth throughout his life. Healthy teeth directly affect overall good health. We already know that bacteria from gum infections can enter the dog's body through the damaged gums and travel to the organs. At a stage in life when his organs don't function as well as they used to, you don't want anything to put additional strain on them. Clean teeth also contribute to a healthy immune system. Offering the dental-type chews in addition to toothbrushing can help, as they remove plaque and tartar as the dog chews.

Along with the same good care you've given him all of his life, pay a little extra attention to your dog in his senior years and keep up with twice-yearly trips to the vet. The sooner a problem is uncovered, the greater the chances of a full recovery.

NORWICH TERRIER

CONFORMATION BASICS

Is dog showing in your blood? Are you excited by the idea of gaiting your handsome Norwich Terrier around the ring to the thunderous applause of an enthusiastic audience? Are you certain that your beloved Norwich Terrier is flawless? You are not alone! Every loving owner thinks that his dog has no faults, or too few to mention. No matter how many times an owner reads the breed standard, he cannot find any faults in his aristocratic companion dog. If this sounds like you, and if you are considering entering your Norwich Terrier in a dog show, here are some basic questions to ask yourself:

• Did you purchase a "show-quality" puppy from the breeder?
• Is your puppy at least six months of age?
• Does the puppy exhibit correct show type for his breed?
• Does your puppy have any disqualifying faults?
• Is your Norwich Terrier registered with the American Kennel Club?
• How much time do you have to devote to training, grooming, conditioning and exhibiting your dog?
• Do you understand the rules and regulations of a dog show?
• Do you have time to learn how to show your dog properly?
• Do you have the financial resources to invest in showing your dog?
• Will you show the dog yourself or hire a professional handler?
• Do you have a vehicle that can accommodate your weekend trips to the dog shows?

Success in the show ring requires more than a pretty face, a waggy tail and a pocketful of liver. Even though dog shows can be exciting and enjoyable, the sport of conformation makes great demands on the exhibitors and the dogs. Winning exhibitors live for their dogs, devoting time and money to their dogs' presentation, conditioning and training. Very few novices, even those with good dogs, will find themselves in the winners' circle, though it does happen. Don't be disheartened,

AKC GROUPS

For showing purposes, the American Kennel Club divides its recognized breeds into seven groups: Terriers, Sporting Dogs, Hounds, Working Dogs, Toys, Non-Sporting Dogs and Herding Dogs.

though. Every exhibitor began as a novice and worked his way up to the Group ring. It's the "working your way up" part that you must keep in mind.

Assuming that you have purchased a puppy of the correct type and quality for showing, let's begin to examine the world of showing and what's required to get started. Although the entry fee into a dog show is nominal, there are lots of other hidden costs involved with "finishing" your Norwich Terrier, that is, making him a champion. Things like equipment, travel, training and conditioning all cost money. A more serious campaign will include fees for a professional handler, boarding, cross-country travel and advertising. Top-winning show dogs can represent a very consider-

able investment—over $100,000 has been spent in campaigning some dogs. (The investment can be less, of course, for owners who don't use professional handlers.)

Many owners, on the other hand, enter their "average" Norwich Terriers in dog shows for the fun and enjoyment of it. Dog showing makes an absorbing hobby, with many rewards for dogs and owners alike. If you're having fun, meeting other people who share your interests and enjoying the overall experience, you likely will catch the "bug." Once the dog-show bug bites, its effects can last a lifetime; it's certainly much better than a deer tick! Soon you will be envisioning yourself in the center ring at the Westminster Kennel Club Dog Show in New York City, competing for the prestigious Best in Show cup. This magical dog show is televised annually from Madison Square Garden, and the victorious dog becomes a celebrity overnight.

Visiting a dog show as a spectator is a great place to start. Pick up the show catalog to find out what time your breed is being shown, who is judging the breed and in which ring the classes will be held. To start, Norwich Terriers compete against other Norwich Terriers, and the winner is selected as Best of Breed by the judge. This is the procedure for each breed. At a group show, all of the Best of Breed winners go on to compete for

BECOMING A CHAMPION

An official AKC championship of record requires that a dog accumulate 15 points under three different judges, including two "majors" under different judges. Points are awarded based on the number of dogs entered into competition, varying from breed to breed and place to place. A win of three, four or five points is considered a "major." The AKC annually assigns a schedule of points to adjust for variations that accompany a breed's popularity and the population of a given area.

Group One in their respective groups. For example, all Best of Breed winners in a given group compete against each other; this is done for all seven groups. Finally, all seven group winners go head to head in the ring for the Best in Show award.

What most spectators don't understand is the basic idea of conformation. A dog show is often referred as a "conformation" show. This means that the judge should decide how each dog stacks up (conforms) to the breed standard for his given breed: how well does this Norwich Terrier conform to the

ideal representative detailed in the standard? Ideally, this is what happens. In reality, however, this ideal often gets slighted as the judge compares Norwich Terrier #1 to Norwich Terrier #2. Again, the ideal is that each dog is judged based on his merits in comparison to his breed standard, not in comparison to the other dogs in the ring. It is easier for judges to compare dogs of the same breed to decide which they think is the better specimen; in the Group and Best in Show ring, however, it is very difficult to compare one breed to another, like apples to oranges. Thus the dog's conformation to the breed standard—not to mention advertising dollars and good handling—is essential to success in conformation shows. The dog described in the standard (the

The ultimate honor in the Norwich's homeland of Britain is success at the prestigious Crufts show.

standard for each American Kennel Club breed is written and approved by the breed's national parent club and then submitted to the American Kennel Club for approval) is the perfect dog of that breed, and breeders keep their eye on the standard when they choose which dogs to breed, hoping to get closer and closer to the ideal with each litter.

Another good first step for the novice is to join a dog club. You will be astonished by the many and different kinds of dog clubs in the country, with about 5,000 clubs holding events every year. Most clubs require that prospective new members present two letters of recommendation from existing members. Perhaps you've made some friends visiting a show held

OTHER TYPES OF COMPETITION

In addition to conformation shows, the AKC holds a variety of other competitive events. Obedience trials, agility trials and tracking trials are open to all breeds, while hunting tests, field trials, lure coursing, herding tests and trials, earthdog tests and coonhound events are limited to specific breeds or groups of breeds. The Junior Showmanship program is offered to aspiring young handlers and their dogs, and the Canine Good Citizen® program is an all-around good-behavior test open to all dogs, pure-bred and mixed.

by a particular club and you would like to join that club. Dog clubs may specialize in a single breed, like a local or regional Norwich Terrier club, or in a specific pursuit, such as obedience, tracking or earthdog tests. There are all-breed clubs for all dog enthusiasts; they sponsor special training days, seminars on topics like grooming or handling or lectures on breeding or canine genetics. There are also clubs that specialize in certain types of dogs, like terriers, hunting dogs, companion dogs, etc.

A parent club is the national organization, sanctioned by the American Kennel Club, which promotes and safeguards its breed in the country. The Norwich and Norfolk Terrier Club can be contacted on the Internet at www.norwichandnorfolkterrier.org. The parent club holds an annual national specialty show in conjunction with the famous all-terrier show in Montgomery County, plus a roving specialty in a different city each year, in which many of the country's top dogs, handlers and breeders gather to compete. At a specialty show, only members of a single breed are invited to participate. There are also group specialties, in which all members of a group are invited. For more information about dog clubs in your area, contact the AKC online at www.akc.org or write them at 5580 Centerview Drive, Raleigh, NC 27606-3390.

OBEDIENCE TRIALS

Mrs. Helen Whitehouse Walker, a Standard Poodle fancier, can be credited with introducing obedience trials to the United States. In the 1930s, she designed a series of exercises based on those of the Associated Sheep, Police, Army Dog Society of Great Britain. These exercises were intended to evaluate the working relationship between dog and owner. Since those early days of the sport in the US, obedience trials have grown more and more popular, and now more than 2,000 trials each year attract over 100,000 dogs and their owners. Any dog registered with the AKC, regardless of neutering or other disqualifications that would preclude entry in conformation competition, can participate in obedience trials.

There are three levels of difficulty in obedience competition. The first (and easiest) level is the Novice, in which dogs can earn the Companion Dog (CD) title. The intermediate level is the Open level, in which the Companion Dog Excellent (CDX) title is awarded. The advanced level is the Utility level, in which dogs compete for the Utility Dog (UD) title. Classes at each level are further divided into "A" and "B," with "A" for beginners and "B" for those with more experience. In order to win a title at a given level, a dog must earn three "legs." A "leg" is accomplished when a dog scores

Dogs shows in which Norwich Terriers can compete are held worldwide, but the rules and standards may vary from country to country.

170 or higher (200 is a perfect score). The scoring system gets a little trickier when you understand that a dog must score more than 50% of the points available for each exercise in order to actually earn the points. Available points for each exercise range from 20 to 40.

A dog must complete different exercises at each level of obedience. The Novice exercises are the easiest, with the Open and finally the Utility levels progressing in difficulty. Examples of Novice exercises are on- and off-lead

JUNIOR SHOWMANSHIP

For budding dog handlers ages 10 to 18 years, Junior Showmanship competitions are an excellent training ground for the next generation of dog professionals. Owning and caring for a dog are wonderful methods of teaching children responsibility, and Junior Showmanship builds upon that foundation. Juniors learn by grooming, handling and training their dogs, and the quality of a junior's presentation of the dog (and himself) is evaluated by a licensed judge. The junior can enter with any registered AKC dog to compete, including an Indefinite Listing Privilege, provided that the dog lives with him or a member of his family.

heeling, a figure-8 pattern, performing a recall (or come), long sit, long down and standing for examination. In the Open level, the Novice-level exercises are required again, but this time without a leash and for longer durations. In addition, the dog must clear a broad jump, retrieve over a jump and drop on recall. In the Utility level, the exercises are quite difficult, including executing basic commands based on hand signals, following a complex heeling pattern, locating articles based on scent discrimination and completing jumps at the handler's direction.

Once he's earned the UD title,

a dog can go on to win the prestigious title of Utility Dog Excellent (UDX) by winning "legs" in ten shows. Additionally, Utility Dogs who win "legs" in Open B and Utility B earn points toward the lofty title of Obedience Trial Champion (OTCh.). Established in 1977 by the AKC, this title requires a dog to earn 100 points as well as three first places in a combination of Open B and Utility B classes under three different judges. The "brass ring" of obedience competition is the AKC's National Obedience Invitational. This is an exclusive competition for only the cream of the obedience crop. In order to qualify for the invitational, a dog must be ranked in either the top 25 all-breeds in obedience or in the top three for his breed in obedience. The title at stake here is that of National Obedience Champion (NOC).

AGILITY TRIALS

Agility trials became sanctioned by the AKC in August 1994, when the first licensed agility trials were held. Since that time, agility certainly has grown in popularity by leaps and bounds, literally! The AKC allows all registered breeds (including Miscellaneous Class breeds) to participate, providing the dog is 12 months of age or older. Agility is designed so that the handler demonstrates how well the dog can work at his side.

TRACKING

Tracking tests are exciting ways to test your Norwich Terrier's instinctive scenting ability on a competitive level. All dogs have a nose, and all breeds are welcome in tracking tests. The first AKC-licensed tracking test took place in 1937 as part of the Utility level at an obedience trial, and thus competitive tracking was officially begun. The first title, Tracking Dog (TD), was offered in 1947, ten years after the first official tracking test. It was not until 1980 that the AKC added the title Tracking Dog Excellent (TDX), which was followed by the title Versatile Surface Tracking (VST) in 1995. Champion Tracker (CT) is awarded to a dog who has earned all three of those titles.

The TD level is the first and most basic level in tracking, progressing in difficulty to the TDX and then the VST. A dog must follow a track laid by a human 30 to 120 minutes prior in order to earn the TD title. The track is about 500 yards long and contains up to 5 directional changes. At the next level, the TDX, the dog must follow a 3- to 5-hour-old track over a course that is up to 1,000 yards long and has up to 7 directional changes. In the most difficult level, the VST, the track is up to 5 hours old and located in an urban setting.

The handler directs his dog through, over, under and around an obstacle course that includes jumps, tires, the dog walk, weave poles, pipe tunnels, collapsed tunnels and more. While working his way through the course, the dog must keep one eye and ear on the handler and the rest of his body on the course. The handler runs along with the dog, giving verbal and hand signals to guide the dog through the course.

The first organization to promote agility trials in the US was the United States Dog Agility Association, Inc. (USDAA). Established in 1986, the USDAA sparked the formation of many member clubs around the country. To participate in USDAA trials, dogs must be at least 18 months of age. The USDAA and AKC both offer titles to winning dogs, although the exercises and requirements of the two organizations differ.

Agility trials are a great way to keep your dog active, and they will keep you running, too! You should join a local agility club to learn more about the sport. These clubs offer sessions in which you can introduce your dog to the various obstacles as well as training classes to prepare him for competition. In no time, your dog will be climbing A-frames, crossing the dog walk and flying over hurdles, all with you right beside him. Your heart will leap every time your dog jumps through the hoop—and you'll be having just as much (if not more) fun!

EARTHDOG EVENTS

Earthdog trials are held for those breeds that were developed to "go to ground." These dogs were bred to go down into badger and fox holes and bring out the quarry. Breeds such as Parson Russell Terriers, Dachshunds and other short-legged hunters, including, of course, the Norwich, are used in this fashion. Earthdog trials test the dog in a simulated hunting situation in which trenches are dug and lined, usually with wood. The scent of a rat is laid in the trench, and the quarry is a caged rat at the end of the tunnel. The dog can see and smell the rat but cannot touch or harm the quarry in any way.

There are four levels in AKC earthdog trials. The first, Introduction to Quarry, is for beginners and uses a 10-foot tunnel. No title is awarded at this level. The Junior Earthdog (JE) title is awarded at the next level, which uses a 30-foot tunnel with three 90-degree turns. Two qualifying JE runs are required for a dog to earn the title. The next level, Senior Earthdog (SE), uses the same length tunnel and number of turns as in the JE level, but also has a false den and exit and requires the dog to come out of the tunnel when called. To try for the SE title, a dog must have at least his JE; the SE title requires three qualifying runs at this level. The most difficult of the earthdog tests, Master Earthdog (ME), again uses the 30-foot tunnel with three 90° turns, with a false entrance, exit and den. The dog is required to enter in the right place and, in this test, honor another working dog. The ME title requires four qualifying runs, and a dog must have earned his SE title to attempt the ME level.

PURPLE AND GOLD HERITAGE

The Westminster Kennel Club show, America's most prestigious dog show, gained its name from the founders' favorite Manhattan hotel bar where they gathered to discuss their sporting ventures. Another theory about the name comes from a Pointer named Juno, who came from the kennel of the Duke of Westminster in England. Although Juno participated in the first show in 1877, the Duke's kennel name likely had less bearing on the choice of the club's name than did the gentlemen's celebrated watering hole. Juno, by the way, is not the Pointer in the Westminster symbol; that Pointer was a celebrated show dog by the name of Sensation, who was owned by the club.

Today the Westminster Kennel Club dog show is the oldest uninterrupted annual dog show in the world, and the second-oldest sporting event in America. The first show was held on May 8–10, 1877 at Gilmore's Garden, the famous Hippodrome, with an entry of over 1,200 dogs. Presently the show is held in the month of February at Madison Square Garden in New York City with an entry of 2,500 champion dogs and is televised nationally.

UNDERSTANDING THE CANINE MINDSET

For starters, you and your dog are on different wavelengths. Your dog is similar to a toddler in that both live in the present tense only. A dog's view of life is based primarily on cause and effect, which is similar to the old saying, "Nothing teaches a youngster to hang on like falling off the swing." If your dog stumbles down a flight of three steps, the next time he will hopefully be more careful, or he may avoid the steps altogether.

Your dog makes connections based on the fact that he lives in the present, so when he is doing something and you interrupt to dispense praise or a correction, a connection, positive or negative, is made. To the dog, that's like one plus one equals two! In the same sense, it's also easy to see that when your timing is off, you will cause an incorrect connection. The one-plus-one way of thinking is why you must never scold a dog for behavior that took place an hour, 15 minutes or even 5 seconds ago. But it is also why, when your timing is perfect, you can teach him to do all kinds of

wonderful things—as soon as he has made that essential connection. What helps the process is his desire to please you and to have your approval.

There are behaviors we admire in dogs, such as friendliness and obedience, as well as those behaviors that cause problems to a varying degree. The dog owner who encounters minor behavioral problems is wise to solve them promptly or get professional help. Bad behaviors are not corrected by repeatedly shouting "No" or getting angry with the dog. Only the giving of praise and approval for good behavior lets your dog understand right from wrong. The longer a bad behavior is allowed to continue, the harder it is to overcome. A responsible breeder is often able to help. Each dog is unique, so try not to compare your dog's behavior with your neighbor's dog or the one you had as a child.

Have your veterinarian check the dog to see whether a behavior problem could have a physical cause. An earache or toothache, for example, could be the reason for a dog to snap at you if you

Digging comes naturally to all terriers, and is even more fun with a friend!

up and abandon your dog. Somewhere a misunderstanding has occurred but, with help and patient understanding on your part, you should be able to work out the majority of bothersome behaviors.

DIGGING

The first problem on every terrier owner's list is digging! Terriers were intentionally bred to be professional diggers, so what could be unnatural or unwanted about your Norwich Terrier's excavating your flower beds? "Nothing!" your Norwich will answer. What is seen as a destructive behavior to us is perfectly natural behavior to terriers, and, in fact, to all dogs. Any dog's desire to dig can be irrepressible and most frustrating to his owners. Terriers dig with more purpose and skill, often incited by the smell of a rodent that passed by a particular mound of dirt. When your Norwich digs with gusto and then sniffs the ground for a moment and continues digging, you know that he is on the trail of some unworthy beady-eyed opponent.

When everyday digging occurs in your yard, it is actually a normal behavior redirected into something the dog can do in his day-to-day life. In the wild, a dog would be actively seeking food, making his own shelter, etc. He would be using his paws in a

were to touch his head when putting on his leash. A sharp correction from you would only increase the behavior. When a physical basis is eliminated, and if the problem is not something you understand or can cope with, ask for the name of a behavioral specialist, preferably one who is familiar with the Norwich Terrier or at least terriers. Be sure to keep the breeder informed of your progress.

Many things, such as environment and inherited traits, form the basic behavior of a dog, just as in humans. You also must factor into his temperament the purpose for which your dog was originally bred. The major obstacle lies in the dog's inability to explain his behavior to us in a way that we understand. The one thing you should not do is to give purposeful manner for his survival. Since you provide him with food and shelter, he has no need to use his paws for these purposes, so the energy that he would be using may manifest itself in the form of little holes all over your yard and flower beds.

For the Norwich Terrier, keeping the dog busy is equivalent to keeping him out of trouble, whether it's digging, barking, chewing or any other problem discussed in this chapter. A bored Norwich fill find something to occupy himself, and likely you will not approve. However, despite his terrier proclivities, an active, occupied Norwich should not be a problem digger.

In the case that a digging problem has developed, digging is easiest to control if it is stopped as soon as possible, but it is often hard to catch a dog in the act. If your dog is a compulsive digger and is not easily distracted by other activities, you can designate an area on your property where he is allowed to dig. If you catch him digging in an off-limits area of the yard, immediately bring him to the approved area and praise him for digging there. Keep a close eye on him so that you can catch him in the act—that is the only way to make him understand what is permitted and what is not. If you take him to a hole he dug an hour ago and tell him "No," he will understand that you are not fond of holes, dirt or flowers. If you catch him while he is stifle-deep in your tulips, that is when he will get your message.

BARKING

Barking is a characteristic bred into the terrier so that the hunter would know where to dig when pursuing quarry. Barking is your Norwich's way of "talking," to communicate his intentions, desires, worries, etc. The smart Norwich's bark is purposeful, not just adding to the cacophony of everyday life. It can be somewhat frustrating to distinguish between a barked message and barked nonsense. It is not always easy for owners to tell what a dog means by his bark—is he excited, frightened, angry or simply enchanted

DOGS OF PREY

Chasing small animals is in the blood of many dogs, perhaps most, and definitely terriers. They think that this is a fun recreational activity (although some are more likely to bring you an undesirable "gift" as a result of the hunt). The good old "Leave it" command works to deter your dog from taking off in pursuit of "prey," but only if taught with the dog on leash for control. Chasing cars, bikes and the like also must be discouraged as this can be dangerous for all parties concerned.

THE MACHO DOG

The Venus/Mars differences are found in dogs, too. Males have distinct behaviors that, while seemingly sex-related, are more closely connected to the role of the male as leader. Marking territory by urinating on it is one means that male dogs use to establish their presence. Doing so merely says, "I've been here." Small dogs often attempt to lift their legs higher on the tree than the previous male. While this is natural behavior outdoors on items like telephone poles, fence posts, fire hydrants and most other upright objects, marking indoors is totally unacceptable. Treat it as you would a house-training accident and clean thoroughly to eradicate the scent. Another behavior often seen in the macho male, mounting is a dominance display. Neutering the dog before six months of age helps to deter this behavior. You can discourage him from mounting by catching the dog as he's about to mount you, stepping quickly aside and saying "Off!"

although, again, boredom can be a cause of nuisance barking.

Excessive habitual barking, when it occurs, is a problem that should be corrected early on. As your Norwich grows up, you will be able to tell when his barking is purposeful and when it is for no reason. You will become able to distinguish your dog's different barks and their meanings. For example, the bark when someone comes to the door will be different from the bark when he is excited to see you. It is similar to a person's tone of voice, except that the dog has to rely totally on tone of voice because he does not have the benefit of using words. An incessant barker will be evident at an early age.

There are some things that encourage a dog to bark. For example, if your dog barks non-stop for a few minutes and you give him a treat to quiet him, he believes that you are rewarding him for barking. He will associate barking with getting a treat and will keep doing it until he is rewarded. On the other hand, if you give him a command such as "Quiet" and praise him after he has stopped barking for a few seconds, he will get the idea that being "quiet" is what you want him to do.

SEPARATION ANXIETY

Any behaviorist will tell you that separation anxiety is the most

by his own voice? If you determine that your Norwich is indeed trying to relay a message, he should not be corrected for barking. It is only when a terrier's barking becomes purposeless and excessive that the behavior needs to be modified. Most Norwich actually use their barks wisely—

common problem about which pet owners complain. It is also one of the easiest to prevent. Unfortunately, a behaviorist usually is not consulted until the dog is a stressed-out, neurotic mess. At that stage, it is indeed a problem that requires the help of a professional.

Training the puppy to the fact that people in the house come and go is essential in order to avoid this anxiety. Leaving the puppy in his crate or a confined area while family members go in and out, and stay out for longer and longer periods of time, is the basic way to desensitize the pup to the family's frequent departures. If you are at home most of every day, make it a point

Most dogs eagerly anticipate their owners' arrival home and are right there at the door to welcome them. This excitement is normal; separation anxiety, however, is a real problem.

PANHANDLING POOCHES

If there's one thing at which dogs excel, it is begging. If there's one thing that owners lack, it's the willpower to resist giving in to their canine beggars! If you don't give in to your adorable puppy, he won't grow into an adult dog that's a nuisance. However, give in just once and the dog will forever figure, "maybe this time." Treats are rewards for correct performance, a category into which begging definitely does not fall. Further, dogs can be clever thieves when food is within their reach, so here's a hint: don't leave food where your Norwich can get it!

to go out for at least an hour or two whenever possible.

How you leave is vital to the dog's reaction. Your dog is no fool. He knows the difference between sweats and business suits, jeans and dresses. He sees you pat your pocket to check for your wallet, open your briefcase, check that you have your cell phone or pick up the car keys. He knows from the hurry of the kids in the morning that they're off to school until afternoon. Lipstick? Aftershave lotion? Lunch boxes? Every move you make registers in his sensory perception and memory. Your puppy knows more about your departures than the

FOUR ON THE FLOOR
You must discourage your dog from jumping up to get attention or for any other reason. To do so, turn away from the dog as he starts to jump up and tell him to sit. "Four on the floor" requires praise. Once the dog sits on command, prevent him from attempting to jump again by asking him to sit/stay before petting him. Back away if he breaks the sit.

FBI ever will. You can't get away with a thing!

Before you got dressed, you checked the dog's water bowl and his supply of long-lasting toys, and turned the radio on low. You will leave him in what he considers his "safe" area, not with total freedom of the house. If you've invested in child safety gates, you can be reasonably sure

that he'll remain in the designated area. Don't give him access to a window where he can watch you leave the house. If you're leaving for an hour or two, just put him into his crate with a safe toy.

Now comes the test! You are ready to walk out the door. Do not give your Norwich Terrier a big hug and a fond farewell. Do not drag out a long goodbye. Those are the very things that jump-start separation anxiety. Toss a biscuit into the dog's area, call out "So long, pooch" and close the door. You're gone. The chances are that the dog may bark a couple of times, or maybe whine once or twice, and then settle down to enjoy his biscuit and take a lovely nap, especially if you took him for a nice long walk after breakfast. As he grows up, the barks and whines will stop because it's an old routine, so why should he make the effort?

When you first brought home the puppy, the come-and-go routine was intermittent and constant. He was put into his crate with a tiny treat. You left (silently) and returned in 3 minutes, then 5, then 10, then 15, then half an hour, until finally you could leave without a problem and be gone for 2 or 3 hours. If, at any time in the future, there's a "separation" problem, refresh his memory by going back to that basic training.

Now comes the next most important part—your return. Do not make a big production of coming home. "Hi, poochie" is as grand a greeting as he needs. When you've taken off your hat and coat, tossed your briefcase on the hall table and glanced at the mail, and the dog has settled down from the excitement of seeing you "in person" from his confined area, then go and give him a warm, friendly greeting. A potty trip is needed and a walk would be appreciated, since he's been such a good dog.

CHEWING

The national canine pastime is chewing, and terriers are built for it! Considering that the Norwich's teeth are, by definition, large and strong, he needs to exercise his God-given endowment. A pup starts chewing when his first set of teeth erupts and continues throughout the teething period. Chewing gives the pup relief from itchy gums and incoming teeth and, from that time on, he gets great satisfaction out of this normal, somewhat idle, canine activity. Providing safe chew toys is the best way to direct this behavior in an appropriate manner. Chew toys are available in all sizes, textures and flavors, but you must monitor the wear-and-tear inflicted on your pup's toys to be sure that the ones you've chosen are safe and remain in good condition.

Puppies cannot distinguish between a rawhide toy and a nice leather shoe or wallet. It's up to you to keep your possessions away from the dog and to keep your eye on the dog. There's a form of destruction caused by chewing that is not the dog's fault. Let's say you allow him on the sofa. One day he takes a rawhide bone up on the sofa and, in the course of chewing on the bone, takes up a bit of fabric. He continues to chew. Disaster! Now you've learned the lesson: Dogs with chew toys have to be either kept off furniture and carpets, carefully supervised or put into their confined areas for chew time.

The wooden legs of furniture are favorite objects for chewing. The first time, tell the dog "Leave it!" (or "No!") and offer him a

FEAR BITING
The remedy for the fear biter is in the hands of a professional trainer or behaviorist. This is not a behavior that the average pet owner should attempt to correct. However, there are things you should not do. Don't sympathize with him, don't pet him and don't, whatever you do, pick him up—you could be bitten in the process, which is even scarier if you bring him up near your face.

"GUARD" DOG

A dog's guarding his dinner dish is totally unacceptable behavior. If your dog starts to exhibit food-guarding tendencies, prevent them by putting part of his food in the dish and picking up the dish when he's finished. Replenish the dish, make him sit and offer him some food from your hand, and then put the dish down. Repeat!

Many dogs extend their guarding impulse toward toys or even items they've stolen. If distracting him from the item doesn't work, try basic obedience. Show a treat and then proceed with calm, slow commands: "Come, Sit, Drop it, Good dog," and then give the treat—positive reinforcement!

chew toy as a substitute. But your clever dog may be hiding under the chair and doing some silent destruction, which you may not notice until it's too late. In this case, it's time to try one of the foul-tasting products, made specifically to prevent destructive chewing, that is sprayed on the objects of your dog's chewing attention. These products also work to keep the dog away from plants, trash, etc. It's even a good way to stop the dog from "mouthing" or chewing on your hands or the leg of your pants. (Be sure to wash your hands after the mouthing lesson!) A little spray goes a long way.

AGGRESSION

"Aggression" is a word that is often misunderstood and is sometimes even used to describe what is actually normal canine behavior. For example, it's normal for puppies to growl when playing tug-of-war. It's puppy talk. There are different forms of dog aggression, but all are degrees of dominance, indicating that the dog, not his master, is (or thinks he is) in control. When the dog feels that he (or his control of the situation) is threatened, he will respond. The extent of the aggressive behavior varies with individual dogs. It is not at all pleasant to see bared teeth or to hear your dog growl or snarl, but these are signs of behavior that, if left uncorrected, can become extremely dangerous. A word of warning here: never challenge an aggressive dog. He is unpredictable and therefore unreliable to approach. Aggression is a concern of all dog owners, even owners of small, friendly dogs like the Norwich.

Nothing gets a "hello" from strangers on the street quicker than walking a puppy, but people should ask permission before petting your dog so you can tell him to sit in order to receive the admiring pats. If a hand comes down over the dog's head and he shrinks back, ask the person to bring their hand up, underneath the pup's chin. Now you're correcting strangers, too! But if you don't, it could make your dog afraid of strangers, which in turn can lead to fear-biting. Socialization prevents much aggression before it rears its ugly head.

The body language of an aggressive dog about to attack is clear. The dog will have a hard, steady stare. He will try to look as big as possible by standing stiff-legged, pushing out his chest, keeping his ears up and holding his tail up and steady. The hackles on his back will rise so that a ridge of hairs stands up. This posture may include the curled lip, snarl and/or growl, or he may be silent. He looks, and definitely is, very dangerous.

This dominant posture is seen in dogs that are territorially aggressive. Deliverymen are constant victims of serious bites from such dogs. Territorial aggression is the reason you should never, ever, try to train a puppy to be a watchdog. It can escalate into this type of behavior over which you will have no control. All forms of aggression must be taken seriously and dealt with immediately. If signs of aggressive behavior continue, or grow worse, or if you are at all unsure about how to deal with your dog's behavior, get the help of a professional.

Uncontrolled aggression, sometimes called "irritable aggression," is not something for the pet owner to try to solve. If you cannot solve your dog's dangerous behavior with professional help, and you (quite rightly) do not wish to keep a canine time-bomb in your home, you will have some important decisions to make. Aggressive dogs often cannot be rehomed successfully, as they are dangerous and unreliable in their behavior. An aggressive dog should be dealt with only by someone who knows exactly the situation that he is getting into and has the experience, dedication and ideal living environment to attempt rehabilitating the dog, which often may not be possible. You cannot pass on to another home a dog that you know could cause harm.

"NIP" IT IN THE BUD

Children can be bitten when they try to retrieve a stolen shoe or toy, so they need to know how to handle the dog or to let an adult do it. They may also be bitten as they run away from a dog, in either fear or play. The dog sees the child's running as reason for pursuit, and even a friendly young puppy will nip at the heels of a runaway. Teach the kids not to run away from a strange dog and when to stop overly exciting play with their own puppy.

INDEX

My Norwich Terrier

PUT YOUR PUPPY'S FIRST PICTURE HERE

Dog's Name _____

Date _____ Photographer _____